UNITED STATES

New Orleans

N

M e

DEC 19

DEC

Washington

UNITED STATES

TEXAS

Austin

New
Orleans

MEXICO

Gulf of Mexico

Tampico

Mexico
City

Veracruz

Puebla

Stephen F. Austin

THEY MADE AMERICA

A series of biographies under the editorship of

Cecile Hulse Matschat   Allan Nevins

Carl Carmer   Lewis Paul Todd

Stephen F. Austin: Father of Texas BY CARLETON BEALS

Charles Willson Peale: Artist and Patriot BY BERTA N. BRIGGS

General Billy Mitchell: Champion of Air
Defense BY ROGER BURLINGAME

George Rogers Clark: Soldier in the West BY WALTER HAVIGHURST

Red Jacket: Last of the Seneca BY ARTHUR C. PARKER

Alexander Hamilton: Nation Builder BY NATHAN SCHACHNER

(Additional books in this series are being prepared.)

Stephen F. Austin

FATHER OF TEXAS

CARLETON BEALS

Drawings by Jay Hyde Barnum

McGraw-Hill Book Company, Inc.

NEW YORK   TORONTO   LONDON

STEPHEN F. AUSTIN: *FATHER OF TEXAS*

Library of Congress Catalog Card Number: 52-13446

Introducing Stephen F. Austin

FEW MEN have accomplished so much in so little time as did Stephen F. Austin, the father of Texas. He explored the Texan wilderness, led in the first settlers, built a new free community, fought a war for independence, and on his deathbed handed to the world a new nation. Few leaders have ever been called upon to perform so many different and difficult tasks.

As a participant in the early westward movement, Austin lived through the hardships of the raw frontier. He fought with Indians and founded new settlements. He journeyed a thousand miles on horseback to Mexico City where, practically without friends or money, he worked a year to persuade the government of Mexico, newly independent of Spain, to revalidate his Spanish land grant for settlers. He journeyed there again numbers of times to fight for the rights of his colonists in Texas, and on one occasion he spent nearly a year in a dark dungeon in solitary confinement. He not only wrote the laws for his colony but helped shape the new constitution of Mexico.

Austin's enterprise called for tireless effort and sacrifice, tact and compromise, firmness and courage. But from the day he first crossed the Sabine River and looked upon that promised land, the word "Texas" was engraved in his heart until he died. To the cause of building a free nation there, he sacrificed love and the simple family life he most craved. When the call came, he took up arms and led the first Texan army of liberation. He raised most of the money for that campaign.

When Texan independence had been achieved, he sacrificed his personal popularity by negotiating with the hated Santa Anna, "the butcher of the Alamo." Thereby, however, he probably saved the new republic from civil war and from new attacks by Mexico. He was called on to conduct the foreign relations of the new nation under the most difficult circumstances, and by the time of his death he had laid the basis for the recognition of Texas by the United States and the other powers.

In a larger sense Austin's efforts led to the eventual acquisition of the entire Southwest and California by the United States. Not only was he the father of Texas; he may be truly called one of the founding fathers of the United States.

CARLETON BEALS

Contents

1 · At the Gates of Texas

IN THE EARLY AFTERNOON of June 26, 1821, the tall stack of the *Beaver* moved in among crowded keelboats and flatboats to the new steamboat landing on Cane River Lake at the north end of Natchitoches in northwestern Louisiana.

Steamboats were now opening up vast stretches of western country, and hordes of people were moving into what had been bow-and-arrow wilderness. A new nation was on the march, and the tide of eager frontiersmen flowed toward the setting sun. They pushed past all obstacles, mountains, forests, rivers, swamps. They defied insects, wild animals, disease, and death. They overran every open space till they came up hard against the great Spanish-built empire. Even after the purchase of Louisiana in 1803,

1

the vast domain of Spain still stretched up through Texas, California, and other western states.

The sleepy Creole inhabitants of the old Spanish-French town of Natchitoches, near the border of Texas, rubbed their eyes at the sight of the big men in boots and spurs and wide hats—men, with long Kentucky rifles, heavy-handed pistols, and cheek wads of tobacco, who flooded in to trade sugar, coffee, knives, and whisky. All up and down the Red River of the South the newcomers were slashing down forests for log-cabin farms and fighting off all comers—Indians, Mexicans, horse thieves, and claim jumpers.

Ever hopeful of lusher, freer country, they gazed across into Catholic New Spain with longing eyes. At the ramparts of that far-flung dominion, with its unwieldy conglomerate of Indians and mestizos of both races, stood the proud sons of Castile, watching with amazement, fear, and hate the land-hungry, westward rush of northern "infidels."

Aboard the *Beaver*, crowding the rail of the clumsy wood-burning craft that hot June day, was a group bound for that bonanza land of New Spain, the wilderness of Texas, outpost of Mexico. Their leader was a young gentleman in a long, dark coat, breeches, and hose.

The heat shimmered across the fields of cotton and corn, and he flicked his fine cambric handkerchief out of his lace sleeve to mop his high, curving forehead. His tall beaver hat was crooked inside his elbow, and the faint breeze ruffled his thick, curly hair. His large, brilliant brown eyes were eager and observant.

Stephen Fuller Austin, yet to reach his twenty-eighth birthday, was about to set forth on his greatest adventure.

To found an American settlement in the forbidding wilds of Texas under the foreign flag of Spain called for courage and willingness to face hardship.

Had he foreseen the endless toil, battles, betrayals, long imprisonment, sickness, and early death, he might have drawn back, though he was not easily swerved from his path. Perhaps he would have returned to New Orleans to resume his law studies and keep on as a well-dressed young blade, welcome at fashionable bars and gay balls.

But "duty" had been a strong word with the Austins ever since an ancestor had settled at New Haven in the early wilderness of Connecticut. Duty now called Stephen to take up the burden that his bankrupt father was about to lay down in disappointment and death. It summoned him to wipe out the family debts and to provide for his mother, younger brother, and sister. Like most pioneers, Steve hoped to make his fortune and was willing to risk his life to succeed.

He little realized, that hot day at the Natchitoches landing, that in following the star of his own hopes, with the restless energy and forthrightness that had always boiled in the blood of the Austins, he would serve far more than his family and himself. He was the spearhead of the great westward urge, the on-rolling power of the new, expanding nation.

Even less did he foresee that he would reshape the destinies of the New World and shift the balance of power everywhere. Just as he did not grasp the terrible difficulties ahead, neither did he vision that he would build up a new empire and strike out boldly, when the day came, for freedom and independence.

He had not been keen about embarking on this enterprise. But having come to a decision, even before he left New Orleans, he had channeled every ounce of will into the project. Now, as he stood erect beside the rail of the *Beaver*, he preferred to dwell on the brighter prospects and even began to look forward with zest to the adventure.

He had first visited Natchitoches three years before, when trading on the Red River. He had seen it again when he poled a flatboat up into the Caddo country of southwest Arkansas to take over the Long Prairie farm and the salt-works his brother-in-law James Bryan had laid out.

As the *Beaver* had pushed past the town, he had noticed again the old Spanish fort and breastworks and the boats packed together in the yellow scum of Bayou Amulet. Long lines of new adobe houses and log cabins had changed the contours of the town.

Above the landing was a rambling, tile-roofed, adobe ranch house. "That belongs to a wealthy family," Steve explained to the lieutenant at his side. "It was built during the first days of Natchitoches by André Chamard. He was a French noble knighted by Louis XVI. One of the Chamard girls is a ravishing beauty."

The lieutenant smiled. "I prefer to pick some dusky belle of the forest. If the Indians try to scalp us, a Pocohontas may come in handy."

Steve smiled wryly, recalling lovely Eliza whom he had known in Lexington, Kentucky, when attending Transylvania University. He had had to drop out of school and go back to Missouri to help salvage his father's lead mines south of St. Louis and had never been able to get back to the bluegrass country. This trip into Texas now made his chances of seeing Eliza again slimmer than ever. He told the lieutenant that he had no intention of marrying until he had paid off the family debts and had gained a foothold on life.

Black slaves gathered up their luggage, and Stephen and his companions pushed through the dock crowd and picked their way around mudholes. Late spring rains had left the streets a sea of red mire.

Telling the others to go to the tavern near Bayou Amulet, Stephen turned up Horn Street to the home of John Sibley, well-known surgeon and Indian agent. A Negro girl opened the big door of the white house, and Stephen passed under the entrance fan of colored glass into the *sala*.

2

John Sibley was a sturdy man, gray at the temples. He greeted Stephen warmly. "We have heard you are going to Texas, and the whole countryside wants to join you. I'd go myself if I weren't so tied down here."

"Wish you could. I'm taking in a couple dozen men to look over the ground."

"Your father told me the details when he got back from that terrible journey of his to San Antonio. Many a younger chap would have hesitated to undertake such a trip. And to pry a settler's concession out of the Spaniards, who are so afraid we want to grab Texas, that was miraculous!"

"He and I were going in together this time, but he is quite ill."

"That rough trip sapped his strength. Those three weeks he was laid up sick with the flux at Hugh McGuffin's ranch left him a scarecrow." Sibley produced some letters. "Here is mail for you, Steve."

Stephen hastened to open the letter from his mother, Maria. It was dated June 8—ten days before he had set out from New Orleans. It had been posted at Hazel Run, Missouri, the home of Stephen's sister, Emily Bryan, near the ill-starred lead mines that had consumed his father's fortune, health, and peace. Steve's eye whisked down his mother's neat handwriting for news of his father.

I have nothing Encouraging to communicate. Dr ben Hiser thought his disorder dangerous, it being a Violent attack of Inflamation of the brest and lungs, attended with a high fever— The Dr staid a day and night blistered and bled most copiously. . . . Your father's fever has returned this day with great violence. he breathes with much difficulty and seems in great distress both in body and mind. . . .

The rest of her letter was more cheerful. His father was surrounded with friends anxious to accompany him to the "Texis" wilds. Emily and her three lovely boys were fine. Little Austin Bryan was very like Stephen. "Laying all parsiality aside," he is "the most interesting child I ever saw—the infant is very butiful."

Stephen told Sibley the news. "I must carry on alone without delay. Mother writes, 'if God in his wisdom thought best to disappoint him'—my father—'in the accomplishment of his wishes and plans formed for the benefit of his family, he prayed Him to extend His goodness to you and enable you to go on with the business in the same way he would have done had not sickness and oh dreadful to think of, perhaps death, prevented him from accomplishing.' "

Stephen's jaw tightened. He had thick, smudge eyebrows, a long, thin, overhanging nose with pinched-in nostrils, and a sensuously curved but firm mouth. Though his features were irregular and one eye cocked up quizzically, he had a strong, sensitive face, handsome at times. At Transylvania many girls had been willing to go up to the "spooning cave" with him.

One rival had carried his jealous spleen to Missouri, where Stephen had become a member of the territorial legislature. Only the efforts of the Masonic lodge had averted a duel.

In Kentucky, Steve's fancy had finally settled on Eliza, but ever since he had left college, his father's tangled affairs had kept him busy. He recalled the time when the boatload of lead he was taking to New Orleans had sunk in the river. They had needed every cent to meet bank notes. Land ventures at Long Prairie and Little Rock, Arkansas, had all but ruined them, and Steve had grown bitter before his time. He had never had the slightest chance to get back to Eliza, and sometimes he felt that he had already lost the most precious thing life had laid before him. But perhaps now, in this riskiest enterprise of all, his luck would change.

He turned to Sibley. "I shall take up where father left off and go right into Texas. Most of the settlers he called on to make the trip have arrived. Some have come long distances. I cannot disappoint them or the others who have contracted to follow us.

"I have a little financial backing—from our good friend Joe Hawkins in New Orleans. He has been an elder brother to me—the finest man alive. The Spanish commissioners from the governor of Texas are already here in Natchitoches to escort our party to San Antonio.

"Our whole family went down with the St. Louis bank crash last year. This is my chance to build everything up again in time, I pray, to provide peace and security to father and the others. This is too great an opportunity to lose—the chance of a lifetime."

Sibley smiled at Steve's frowning earnestness. "I hope all goes as you expect. I can give you some good pointers. I have been part way over the San Antonio Trace several times."

"I've already looked over your book on the Louisiana Indians," replied Steve.

"The information was prepared especially for my friend President Jefferson. I have many notes on the Texas Indians, too."

Stephen rubbed his hat with his sleeve and turned to leave. He was going to the house of the local Spanish agent, where he would pay his respects to Señor José Erasmo Seguín, the special representative of the governor of Texas.

The agent was a slim man of French extraction, but Don Erasmo was a rough-hewn, bulletheaded Creole of the frontier. Though earthly and blunt, he had the inborn courtesy of his race and impressed Steve with respect and confidence.

Don Erasmo called in his assistant, Juan Martín de Veramendi, and several Spanish merchants. Veramendi was an elegant, austere aristocrat, a personage of wealth and consequence.

All were presented to Steve with great formality and

resounding phrases that rolled forth like music—a polished etiquette more like that of the royal court than the rough frontier and very different from the breezy shoulder slapping of western Americans. Though accustomed since boyhood, in Missouri and New Orleans, to elaborate Latin politeness, Steve knew it was going to require patient tact to deal with these people who refused to be rushed and loved fine manners.

Steve presented to Don Erasmo an engraved silver dagger that he had purchased in New Orleans. It was said to have belonged to Jean Laffite, the French pirate who had recently been driven out of his Galveston hide-out by United States frigates.

Don Erasmo's dark eyes lighted up with pleasure. "Your father was a sterling gentleman who won the firm friendship of all, from the governor down, and his son, I now observe, is cut from the same fine cloth."

He was pleased that Stephen was going ahead with the venture. "Our government has been greatly alarmed by the armed filibuster expeditions from your country, but we welcome peaceful settlers. We are anxious to build up the province rapidly with good farms and industry. That will put an end to lawless armed raids and help us save Texas.

"Part of my mission here is to invite all Spaniards who fled from Texas at the time of the early independence revolt to return with full pardons. The governor is offering free lands to all who will do so. I have already collected quite a party to go back with us. Spain has just adopted a new liberal constitution that guarantees freedom for all."

Seguín urged haste. The Austin land grant still had to be ratified by the Spanish viceroy in far-off Mexico City. This was a mere formality, but conditions were unsettled.

The movement to free Mexico from Spain, begun ten years earlier, had never been wholly stamped out. Once more it was sweeping through town after town. Four months ago Crown General Agustín Iturbide, a glittering daredevil, ladies' man, and gambler, had betrayed the viceroy by joining up with the revolutionists he had been sent to suppress. The viceroy was in hot water, and Seguín urged Steve to obtain his final ratification before civil war made it impossible and to start his settlement quickly.

Rejoining his companions for supper at the inn, Steve showed them the thick parchment handed to him so ceremoniously by Seguín. Dated January 17, 1821, at the capitol in Monterrey, the message on the parchment told all concerned that Moses Austin, Steve's father, had been granted the right to settle 300 families on 200,000 acres on the Colorado and Brazos rivers at the head of San Bernardo Bay. All immigrants had to be Catholics or had to accept Catholicism, and they had to take the oath of allegiance to the Spanish crown and constitution. Moses Austin guaranteed that all settlers would be "honest industrious farmers and mechanics."

Confident this grant would stand up as legal with any government that might in the future rule in Mexico, Steve sketched out a call for settlers to come to Texas.

"Liberal privileges are secured both in regard to commercial intercourse and civil rights." The "beneficial results" of the new Spanish constitution are "already perceptible."

3

Again Steve thought over his first trip to Natchitoches, when he had come trading along the Red River for James Bryan. Moses Austin, already hoping to get a Texas land grant, had suggested that Bryan take up the Caddo claim as a jumping-off place for settlers making the hard trek across the Texas plains.

The Long Prairie farm was in fine open country, carpeted with rich grass and vivid with wild flowers, but it was too difficult to reach. No steamer could get through the river above Natchitoches, and even large keelboats had difficulty. In low-water season Steve and his slave Richmond had spent four days rigging up a windlass to pull their boat across the rock-ledge rapids. It had taken thirty days to make 90 miles through the Big Raft where the river widened into a swamplike lake close-clogged with driftwood. To pry 30 feet through one log jam took the whole day. Clouds of waterfowl rose screaming. They ran into alligators and poisonous water moccasins.

Steve had tried to make a go of the Long Prairie place, but through tricky rulings the titles had been made defective. He sold everything and rode his gray horse to Little Rock, the new capital of Arkansas, to engage in land speculation.

Tricked again on titles and by his father's partner in the St. Louis bank, he lost all and was saddled with a $7,000 debt. He refused a political appointment in Arkansas and went to New Orleans with only the clothes on his back. There Joseph Hawkins, brother of a friend

Steve had known while at the university, generously took him into his family—a wife and five young children—and provided him with clothes, food, and lodging. He even gave him money so that he could send groceries north to his mother and sister, hard pressed while Moses was away in Texas. Hawkins soon got him a job as editor of the Louisiana *Advertiser*.

Steve wrote his mother that this kind help at such a dark moment had made him change his opinion of the human race. Now Hawkins was helping with the Texas business.

4

With the lieutenant and another friend, Steve went down to Bayou Amulet to buy animals and supplies. It was a busy, bawling scene, jostle and jabber—English, Spanish, French, and Indian. Negroes were rolling hogsheads of rum or whisky, maneuvering bales of cotton, or toting sacks of flour, coffee, and sugar on or off the boats jammed in the inlet. They sang lilting chanties in rhythm with their smooth-flowing muscles.

Big cavalcades of mules and horses were coming in, loaded with Mexican silver, hides, and dried buffalo tongues. Other trains of animals were being loaded with whisky, tobacco, firearms, powder, salt, flour, cloth, hardware.

The Mexican mule drivers were a hardy, picturesque breed in thonged sandals, big wide sombreros, white drill trousers with scarlet sashes, knives, and pistols. They lived a dangerous life, freighting through savage Indian country, exposed to attacks from reckless bandits and horse thieves. Mostly short swarthy mestizos, they were tough and happy-go-lucky and helped shoot up saloons and dives in Natchitoches and La Bahía.

Steve dickered for three pack mules and bought a French saddle and a long-barreled rifle, for they would have to hunt much of their food. They purchased flour, corn, leather canteens, knives, powder, and shot.

Some of his party failed to arrive. By candlelight he pored over the papers that Sibley had lent him. The Indian tribes in East Texas had a host of odd names. The tall, powerful Karankawa handled stiff 6-foot bows that no white man could bend and shot their long, steel-tipped arrows with the range and accuracy of firearms. They and the Coco were said, perhaps falsely, to be cannibals.

In New Orleans a member of a filibuster expedition told Steve that he got along marvelously with the big brown Karankawa chief. But the Karankawa's nomadic habits, thieving, and raiding, Steve feared, would make it impossible to Christianize them, as the French had the Caddo around Natchitoches.

Everybody that Steve saw, wished to go with him to Texas. He told all that they should not expect to make money quickly; all they would have would be a humble home built by their own labor, but they would be free and independent. What was more important than that? Here in the New World man's happiness was promoted by subduing the wilderness by the ax, the plow, and the hoe.

For the next few days Steve wiped his brow in the heat and fumed. He was most eager to start, for several adventurous bands, mostly reckless riffraff, were recruiting in New Orleans for armed expeditions. Before Steve left that city, he had been approached by General José Félix Trespalacios, who had asked Steve to join with him. The general promised land, money, and loot in the name of freeing Mexico from Spain. Steve told him that, although the Austin land grant had been made by the Spanish king, it had been ratified by the elected representatives of the people; he intended to support whatever legal government controlled the country. Trespalacios threatened that his revolutionaries would never recognize the grant. Steve feared that Trespalacios might cause future trouble for him, and he was anxious to get his colonizing under way before he was blocked.

But not till July 2 did his second group put in an appearance. It was headed by Edward Lovelace, of New Orleans, a reliable man ready to put money behind the expedition.

Steve sent his entire party ahead under Lovelace. He waited for Seguín and his men to set out. In a few days he would be on his way to the Sabine River and on through Texas to fabulous San Antonio. He had accomplished in a few weeks what his father had failed to accomplish in many months, and he prayed that he would be more successful in his quest.

2 · Into the Wilds

STEVE RODE OUT OF NATCHITOCHES alone on his old gray
horse and caught up with his party near Hugh McGuffin's
ranch. McGuffin turned over to him belongings left there
by his father, including a tomahawk that Moses had used
to mark trees on his way to San Antonio. Stephen hefted it.
"I shall cherish this, for it has blazed the trail for thousands
more sure to follow."

McGuffin told Steve of his father's bad luck. Moses had
started back from San Antonio with an American who stole
all his supplies and animals. He and his young Negro slave
had had to walk eight days on foot. Their powder got damp
from rain and the swollen streams that they had crossed
on logs. As a result they could shoot no game and had to
live on roots and acorns. A panther jumped out of a tree on
Moses when he was sleeping, but he managed to scramble
free.

15

"He was a gaunt shadow and a sick man when he staggered into my place."

Near the Sabine River frontier a courier brought Steve word that his father had died. Shocked and sad, he sent his party across into Texas but waited in vain at a ranch for Don Erasmo to catch up with the mail. Finally, impatient and sick at heart, Steve raced back to Natchitoches only to find that he had missed Don Erasmo. He penned a letter to his mother.

Only those who had been "in this wild country" could have any idea of the suffering his father had gone through. But we "must resign ourselves to the dispensations of Providence, death must finally terminate the career of us all." He paused, thinking back over the years.

Moses Austin had been a stern man. Sometimes his quick, wild temper made him do cruel, thoughtless things, but he was warmhearted and instantly contrite. However, his contrition did not always bring back alienated friends or heal family resentments. His ideas were always more grandiose than his abilities. Most of his ventures, after brief success, had ended in failure. Each time he had moved farther into the wilderness.

As a young man he had gone from Durham, Connecticut, to Philadelphia to start a business. There he had married a New Jersey girl, Maria Brown. He had gone on to work lead mines in southern Virginia.

Stephen had been born there, November 3, 1793; and a few years later, his sister Emily. When the Virginia enterprise faded out, Moses led his family into the Indian wilds of Missouri, then under Spanish rule. There the third child, James, had been born a Spanish subject.

For a time Moses' lead mines had prospered, but a mountain of debt had accumulated. He had started a bank in St. Louis, but it failed, wiping out his resources completely. At the twilight of his life he had taken the long, long trail to Texas—and to death.

Moses had made sacrifices to give his children a good education. When eleven, Stephen had been sent to the Bacon Academy in Colchester, Connecticut, then supervised by the notable teacher, John Adams. Moses had written Adams that he wanted Stephen to know the classics yet not waste too much time on Greek and Hebrew. Though not the sort of parent to force his son into a particular occupation, he wished the boy to become a practical businessman and lawyer. Above all, Steve was to be taught to think freely and not become a bigot either in politics or in religion.

Moses had wished Stephen to go on to Yale but was obliged to send him to the new college in the West—Transylvania—where living was cheaper.

Thinking warmly of these things, Stephen picked up his pen again. "He was one of the most . . . affectionate fathers that ever lived," he wrote his mother. "His faults I now say, and always have, were not of the heart."

Moses' death made Steve aware of man's short span, and he wrote, "I pray you to be careful of your tender health. I hope to embrace my dear Mother and Sister once more next fall."

2

July 16, 1821, Stephen Fuller Austin set foot on Texas soil for the first time. Then, as later, he looked about with eager eyes and made notes on every step of the journey:

timber, soil, what crops would flourish; navigable rivers, which ones could turn the wheels of future mills; where mines could be dug; towns laid out. He foresaw populous cities, prosperous farms, a free, happy community—the great American dream.

The following day he made a side trip to a ranch recently started in the wilds by Josiah H. Bell. Bell had been Steve's agent in the Long Prairie days. He had had much experience with Mexicans and would be of great help to the new colony.

"Come in with us," Steve urged. "I can promise you a generous grant of land and a position of authority. You can fix yourself up for life and very likely make a fortune."

Steve overtook his company near Nacogdoches. This town, beautifully situated on elevated ground in heavily timbered country, was dry and healthy. Once it had been the seat of prosperous Indian trade. Of the original buildings only a stone church and a large stone house were left standing.

It now had only a hundred rough-and-tumble inhabitants —Spaniards, French, Americans, Indians, free Negroes, and slaves—living in adobe huts or log cabins. The alcalde, or mayor, was an American named James Dill. Seguín assembled all able-bodied males to give them instructions from the governor. All North American settlers were asked to move inland from the border. They would be given liberal land grants deeper in Texas.

Steve and his men rode on through gently rolling country resembling the barrens of Kentucky. Soon they left behind them the last two settlers on the whole long Camino Real—"Royal Highway"—to San Antonio.

"We had better keep our two parties close together from here on," suggested Seguín.

Several overland parties from La Bahía reported three scalped bodies on the trail, one Mexican and two Americans. Warily Austin's men crossed a wide, smooth prairie with the highest, thickest grass Steve had ever seen. The deep river soil was jet black with signs of iron pyrites. The bottoms of the wide Trinity were so dense that it was eleven o'clock that night before they got across the stream and could eat. Fear of Indians caused them to keep their horses herded together.

The sentry on the second watch yelled an alarm. Everybody jumped to his gun and shot wildly at two motionless Indians, on white horses, silhouetted above the bluff. No one slept all night.

Daylight seeped over the silver dew on the prairie with the call of wild turkeys and mourning doves. Sheepishly the men saw the watchful Indians firmly "fixed in the ground"—stumps and tree roots!

On August 4 they killed their first buffalo and the next day came upon big herds. Three days later, at the broad Colorado, they were amazed by the miles on miles of wild vines yielding large, well-flavored grapes. "Good for making red wine," Steve observed.

There were many pecans and considerable ash, oak, and cedar. Near the San Marcos River the soil was black and rich, but there was no timber, only mesquite and grass. "Water is scarce but good," he recorded in his notes.

3

Seguín sent three men ahead to San Antonio to advise the governor to prepare quarters for the Americans. The messengers returned on August 12 with "glorious news." The Texan authorities had announced the independence of Mexico.

The Mexicans in Austin's party danced around like crazy men, shouting, *"Viva la Independencia!"* They raced their horses madly, raising clouds of dust, shooting, and yelling.

Seguín invited Stephen to breakfast with him on dishes sent out to the men by their wives in San Antonio: *tortillas,* beans, rice, barbecued meat, all highly seasoned.

He leaned back soberly. "We are Mexicans now, and God help us! We are free, a tremendous change—*tremendo!* Now we can build a great free nation. Do you realize Mexico will be the third largest country in the world? Only China and Russia are bigger."

"But none of it is greater than Texas," said Stephen fervently. "Its fertility and resources exceed anything I ever dreamed of. It will become a rich progressive state, and I am determined to devote my life to redeeming it from the wilderness. It will become the brightest jewel of the whole Mexican crown. I shall be proud to be a citizen of such a great free country."

Seguín was deeply moved.

3 · Exploring the Grant

SUN-DRENCHED SAN ANTONIO wore a tawny gown of faded glory. On the handsome central military plaza stood the governor's palace and the magnificent San Fernando Cathedral. Notables dwelt in fine stone houses with delightful flowering patios and terraces. Under the arcades were numerous commercial establishments. Four were run by Frenchmen; several, by Americans.

In this golden compact square the worship of God, the power of the state, and the handicrafts of man were centered—a unity featuring ideal Spanish city planning everywhere.

From its impressive center the city faded off through narrow streets to mestizo and Indian adobe and thatched huts, with vivid white, blue, or pink walls, set in gardens behind cactus fences. Irrigation ditches, often neatly tiled, ran to gardens and farms.

21

San Antonio had about 5,000 people, but for some years it had not progressed. The original grandeur had not been matched by later achievements. Some older buildings had fallen into ruin. South across the plain were four massive missions, their towers and cupolas poking into the hot, hazy sky, but one had been abandoned. The Alamo, too, was half in ruins, its roof gone, the chapel boarded up, the crumbling interior filled with broken bricks and rubbish. Weeds and vines, lodged in crevices, softened the old yellow-brown walls, giving it an air of sad decay.

Governor Antonio de Martínez provided the weary travelers with good quarters on the square. Steve put up at Seguín's house, a rambling adobe ranch with an inner patio and back corrals. Married to a buxom mestiza, Seguín had three children in their teens.

Steve's first visitor was Baron de Bastrop, a genial, stocky Dutchman, who had helped arrange the original land grant for Moses. A clever, adventurous promoter, Bastrop had known high estate in Europe but had had to flee from revolution and war. In the United States and then in Texas, his engaging personality and keen intelligence won him instant friendship and confidence. He was close to the Spanish authorities.

Over a glass of brandy Bastrop told of Moses' difficult experiences the year before. On his arrival in San Antonio, Moses and two other Americans had been ordered out of the city and the province instantly. The authorities were touchy over invasions by filibusters, and American smugglers were supposed to be stirring up the Comanches and other Indians. Moses showed Bastrop his early Spanish passport to Missouri and claimed that his youngest son,

James Austin, born on Spanish soil, was a citizen of the empire. He was a Catholic. When the baron took Moses straight to Governor Martínez, the latter proved more reasonable. If Moses would make formal application for a land grant, Martínez would recommend it to the superior authorities at Monterrey. Even so, Moses would have to return to the United States and wait there for an answer.

Equally helpful to Steve, Bastrop now took him to see Martínez. Before the handsome palace two cockaded sentries, in blue and scarlet uniforms, paced with lifted swords and methodical heel clicks. The entrance keystone bore the date 1749. Bastrop said that one wing had been put up much earlier as a presidio, or barracks.

Governor Martínez received them cordially—a portly, dark-eyed official in velvet breeches and coat, a lace-frilled shirt, white stockings, and silver-buckled shoes. He had already received favorable reports of Stephen and his party from Seguín and his Natchitoches agent.

"Until regular administration can be set up, the colony should be wholly under my command," suggested Stephen. "That's the only way it will work." The governor agreed and promised to have the plan approved by his superiors.

Steve figured out a way to control the Indian trade, to halt raiding and smuggling, and to provide government revenues. New military posts should be set up, and trade should be put into the hands of authorized agents or companies. An agreement to prevent smuggling should be made with the United States.

Seguín and Bastrop believed that the plan would be workable and profitable.

Stephen departed to explore the Colorado region. He

intended to look over his vast grant to determine where the first settlements should be made. The governor, Baron de Bastrop, and Seguín graciously accompanied him and his men for the first day. Uniformed aides, cavalrymen in blue with scarlet cockades, outriders, servants, and others made it "a kingly cavalcade." But the next morning, after affectionate farewells, Austin and his men continued alone over the old Opelousas Trace to Rancho de las Arrochas.

Here they met Gocosa, a Karankawa chief, clad in beaded, fringed buckskin and soft deerskin moccasins. A bright woven band held back his flowing, long black hair. With him were three subchiefs and ten squaws clad in homespun red skirts, wide scarlet sashes, and sleeveless embroidered blouses. Bright necklaces circled their dusky throats.

Stephen smoked peace tobacco, and Gocosa sent word to the nearest village that the travelers were to be treated properly. After the dreadful tales he had heard about this tribe, Stephen was glad to find it so hospitable.

The next day the village Indians caught up with them. Stephen gave them tobacco but scarcely paused. This conduct angered the chief, and the Indians dogged the travelers for 10 miles, begging insolently.

La Bahía, later called Goliad, was beautifully situated on the San Antonio River. "The surrounding country is rolling prairie, rather sandy but it produces well, and all could be watered from the River," Steve wrote.

On September 4, a cloudy, windy day, they rode through oak and pecan groves to the high bluffs of the Guadalupe River. Alligators slid off the mudbanks with heavy splashes. The men caught a big fish and fat soft-shelled turtles and shot a large buck. They saw a herd of 400 deer and 150 mustangs. Later, beside a large lake, they came upon an abandoned Karankawa settlement and soon reached the head of the San Antonio branch of scenic Matagorda Bay. The west bank was heavily wooded, but the 25-foot east bank extended back to a great prairie.

"What a beautiful situation for a town!" exclaimed Steve.

As they went on, Steve blazed the trails with his father's old tomahawk until finally they reached the Brazos, the most magnificent spot yet. Steve's eyes kindled. Here was another fine place for a town. Here someday a great city would rise—farms, houses, factories, a whole new world to be.

North for 150 miles the country was equally marvelous, "the best land in the whole province. . . . It is good for farming, lumbering and industries. The climate is superb . . . a paradise . . . the finest country in all the world."

Here he would plant his colony. His father Moses had not been able to lead his chosen people to the "Promised Land," but Stephen vowed that he would shape here a new life in freedom.

2

The expedition got back to Natchitoches on October 1. Stephen saw Sibley, the Spanish agent, and others. Then he returned to Nacogdoches to talk with settlers wishing to go to his colony. He sent in fifty families. He saw Josiah Bell again and clinched a final deal.

"Subject to Governor Martínez's approval, I'm appointing you justice of the peace," he told Josiah and granted him 960 acres plus 320 for his wife, 320 for each of his two children, and 160 for each of his three slaves.

Such large grants were not what the midwestern small farmers, who cultivated their own soil were accustomed to. They were in the tradition of the southern plantation manned by slaves.

Steve made a detailed report for Governor Martínez. "The land . . . I have selected on which to locate the new colony, is situated on the Colorado and the Brazos from their mouths to six leagues above the Upper San Antonio Road." Unable to decide upon a port, he was going to outfit a boat in New Orleans to study the coast as far as the Guadalupe River; then he would return overland to San Antonio to report his findings.

The following day he wrote a more personal letter to the governor. In it he suggested that the government appoint an agent to help locate the settlers and issue titles to land, so that they would not have to make long, expensive trips to San Antonio.

"I have a hundred new inquiries from people eager to take up land and I could settle fifteen hundred families as easily as three hundred." He suggested that his grant be extended to the Guadalupe and San Marcos rivers on the west and the Trinity and San Jacinto rivers on the east.

His dreams and ambitions were growing.

4 · Starting the Settlement

REACHING NEW ORLEANS, Steve went directly to the home of Joe Hawkins. Georgia Hawkins and the children were delighted. The older boy, about twelve, was fair and straight, but Edmund St. John was dark, aggressive, and given to quick resentments. The three girls were pretty little kittens.

Steve brought them Indian trinkets, plaited horsehair belts, and bright woven sashes; and for Georgia, a Mexican topaz brooch.

Steve told Joe that the wealth of Texas surpassed his wildest dreams. "The idea of filling it with an industrious, civilized population fires my soul with enthusiasm!" he exclaimed. His glowing account made Joe anxious to invest every cent he could in the enterprise.

They drew up a formal contract. Steve acknowledged receipt of $4,000, most still to be paid in. Hawkins would receive half the land that Stephen would be awarded as *empresario*—63,000 acres—and half the net profits.

From Lovelace, who had come to New Orleans with him, Steve obtained $500 on the promise that he would try to obtain a land grant around Galveston Bay in which each would have a half interest.

They bought and outfitted the *Lively*, a small vessel with which to explore the coast and get the colony started. Steve put up two-thirds of the cost; Hawkins, one-third. For a crew Steve contracted thirteen men with arms to remain in his employ till December, 1822. They agreed to obey orders and to conduct themselves as loyal citizens. They were to take soundings of the coast, build cabins and stockades, and plant at least 5 acres of corn each. Austin guaranteed to provide farming tools, oxen or mules, provisions, and seed. On fulfilling the contract, each would get half the crops he had raised plus a 640-acre tract of land and a town lot.

As civil commander of the colony, Steve had printed up the conditions for settlement. Land occupied and partly cultivated by January, 1823, would be delivered free of all fees and surveying costs on payment of 12½ cents an acre. Mechanics and men of capital would be allowed additional land and privileges "in proportion to their capacity to be useful."

Steve hurried north to Natchitoches to lay in supplies: blue strouding (a coarse cloth much prized by the Indians), blankets, axes, powder, flints, sugar, coffee, and biscuits.

He interviewed more settlers and answered applications

from all sorts: schoolteachers, ministers, lawyers, doctors, veterinarians, dentists, politicians, and plain ordinary folk, most of whom knew nothing of woodcraft or farming.

His mother sent word that James had been very sick. But now, only two days out of bed, he was heading for Texas. She feared that, like his father, he would "anticipate a thousand pleasing projects" that he would "never realize." But he had "in a measure got the better of that warmth of temper he formerly had" and now has the "prudence to govern" his "high spirit . . . with reason and propriety." He has a "strong and active mind, capable and willing to encounter difficulty and danger—I hope he will be of service to you my much beloved Son." She, her daughter, and grandchildren all expected to come to Texas in the fall. She planned to bring Moses' body along.

Steve reached Nacogdoches in mid-December and proceeded to the Brazos. Several families were already camped at the La Bahía road crossing, near present-day Washington, and on nearby creeks. Rival Indian tribes, massacring each other 30 miles north, kept them alarmed, and the drought was so bad that they had harvested less corn than they had planned. They were living entirely on venison and honey.

With ten men Steve hurried on to the mouth of the Colorado, where he was to meet the *Lively*. The ship failed to show up.

All January and February, Austin's party moved hither and yon around great Matagorda Bay, scanning the purple-blue water anxiously. They pushed through swamps and forests and dense evergreen thickets bright with red berries. Their food gave out and their powder was spoiled;

they had to subsist on catfish and wild onions. Steve finally gave up the vessel, supplies, and crew as lost. This was a grievous setback, and his friends aboard her, Lovelace and others, might have perished.

But upcountry at the La Bahía crossing, Stephen was consoled by the arrival of his brother James. He could now count fifty settlers on the Brazos and a hundred on the Colorado driving pegs into new cabins, planting corn, getting ready for their families already on the road.

2

March 3 he and James left with twenty men for San Antonio. The trip was hard, but the spring growth was beautiful: glowing-eyed daisies, tall sunflowers, hill slopes aflame with mountain pinks. Whole prairies were carpeted with buffalo clover, which later settlers called "bluebells." These flowers changed the prairie into an inverted sky, stretching to the far horizon, heaven to heaven.

Bad news met them. The provincial government at Monterrey had overruled Governor Martínez and had ordered Austin not to distribute lands, appoint judges, or assume any authority whatever. Settlers could be put provisionally on land designated by the nearest *ayuntamiento*, or municipal government, but each case had to be referred to distant Monterrey. Endless delay and red tape would wreck everything.

"The Monterrey people simply don't realize what a big task we are undertaking," Steve told Martínez hotly. "Families come 1,000 miles or more overland, enough to shake the stamina of the strongest, often fatal for women and children. Weary, provisions gone, they have to pitch right in to fell trees, dress lumber, and build cabins. They have to fight off Indians, clear the land, plow, cultivate, and seed the fields—all in a few short months. At such a ticklish time, how are they going to worry about titles? Before anything they had to keep from starving. How can they travel 700 miles more to Monterrey, leaving their families at the mercy of hunger and Indians, and wait around for weeks, maybe months, where they know no one and do not speak the language? How many will want to make improvements unless sure they will keep their land and their homes?"

"If I were certain to stay on here as governor," Martínez replied, "I would tell you to go right ahead, and we'd gradually get everything straightened out. But my days here are numbered. Great changes have occurred."

In Mexico City destiny had marched ahead violently and bloodily. Juan O'Donojú, the Spanish viceroy, had been halted at Veracruz and forced to sign the Pact of Córdoba recognizing Mexican independence, and Iturbide had entered the capital triumphantly as "Liberator" at the head of troops bearing the new green-white-and-red flag of freedom. While Stephen was off beating the brush in search of the *Lively*, Mexico's first Independence Congress met on February 24, 1822.

"Mexico is really independent now," Martínez continued. "It will demand new men. I'm a Spaniard born in Spain. From now on you will have to deal with the Creoles [Spaniards native to Mexico] and with the mestizos [the men of mixed blood]. They will suspect everything done by the old regime; they will throw out even good officials."

"How will that affect my concession?" asked Stephen.

"You must hasten to Mexico City and get your grant revalidated, or you may bring hardship and disappointment to your settlers."

3

No moment could have been worse for Steve to absent himself from the colony. A thousand urgent matters had to be attended to. Bell, who had settled on the Brazos, wrote him that new colonists were "crowding" in daily, even settling on land that Stephen had staked out for himself. "These colonists should be given permanent farms to build homes and get in quick crops lest they starve. Differences have to be ironed out or things will soon be in a bad tangle."

Steve wished that Baron de Bastrop were around to advise him, but his friend had gone to the capital. At least Steve would have one friend in that unknown city.

He was not prepared for such a long, costly journey. He fingered the $350 in gold doubloons in his money belt—all he had in the world. It was not nearly enough. He could not afford to take James along.

At an elaborate dinner at the governor's house with Erasmo Seguín and others, all offered to lend James a hand. Martínez's plump black-eyed wife and her charming sister were especially sympathetic, and Seguín insisted that James live in his home. He was furious at the mere mention of any payment.

His friends warned Steve that the trip would be dangerous. The countryside was swarming with bandits and Indians on the warpath. Hungry demobilized soldiers roamed about, recklessly looting and killing.

When Dr. Robert Andrews and a friend offered to go along, the journey promised to be safer and more pleasant. Andrews, just arrived in San Antonio, had gone into the Caddo country with Steve and Bryan. Besides being a physician, he was a surveyor, hunter, trapper, member of the Arkansas legislature, and Jack-of-all-trades. His great spirit of good-humored adventure made him a fine man to have along.

Steve received his visa to depart on March 13 but for greater safety postponed departure to join a large cavalcade of Mexicans setting out for Monterrey.

5 · South to the Halls of Montezuma

THE COUNTRYSIDE BELOW SAN ANTONIO was barren. The blazing sun shimmered across desolate sands sprinkled sparsely with mesquite and palo blanco and broken only here and there by solitary red buttes. Organ cactus rose in great pillars like ruined stone cities. Lizards and horned toads scuttled out of their way. Under the alamos of a dry watercourse, a Gila monster came spitting at them, hood angrily lifted. Rattlesnakes coiled, singing under the horses' hoofs, and at night the travelers slept inside several turns of horsehair *reatas* to keep reptiles off.

Andrews, not young any more, coughed constantly from lung trouble, and the dust from their horses made him jack-knife in his saddle.

Impatient at being held back by the heavily laden Mexican cavalcade, the three Americans dashed ahead and camped alone 6 miles from the Nueces River.

In the morning Andrews and his friend, Dr. Waters, advised against making a fire to prepare breakfast lest it betray them to Indians. Steve said he would make only a small fire in a side gully while they rounded up the horses.

Hearing hoofbeats, he reached for his gun. Fifty Comanches galloped upon him with wild whoops, their spears glistening in the early sun. They whirled around him in two semicircles. He stood on the saddles, hoping to save them.

The band fell on their possessions greedily, ripping open bundles, scattering things around, and yelling with glee over prized objects.

Another group of Indians brought in Andrews and Waters and their three horses.

With a twist of his mouth, Andrews said in English, "Say your prayers, gentlemen, and do hold on to your scalps."

Using the few words of Comanche that he knew, Steve asked the chief if his nation was at war with Americans.

"No."

"Do you like Americans?"

"Yes, they are our friends."

"Where do you get your spearheads, your blankets?"

"Get them from our friends, the Americans."

"If you were passing through our country, would you be robbed this way?"

The chief reflected. "No, it would not be right."

To Steve's astonishment all the stolen goods, except four blankets, a bridle, several small objects, and a Spanish grammar that the chief asked to keep, reappeared magically. But, to his dismay, he noticed that the saddle-bags, containing all their money, had not been returned.

Rushing over to a squaw beating a mustang in the under-brush, Steve found the bags concealed under her saddle blanket. When he wrenched them away from her, all laughed gleefully at her angry sputtering.

Shortly after this, some traders saw the grammar in the possession of an Indian and read Stephen's name on the flyleaf. They spread the word that he had been killed. Many colonists were dismayed and returned to the United States. James wrote the sad news home to Missouri. Steve's mother and sister mourned his death for nearly four months.

2

For days Austin and his friends toiled across barren, brittle country. Low ridges narrowed purple and red toward the Santa Catalina Valley. The big Monterrey cathedral rose bold and tawny against a triple-cleft mountain. High on lone Chepa Vera Hill, the bishop's palace stood like a medieval castle above thatched and adobe shacks and open-air eating places.

"Monterrey is an old, old city," a Mexican companion told them. "Its Plaza de Armas was laid out in 1579."

When Steve went for his visa, the authorities were uneasy about the dramatic struggle going on in the center of the country. None was sure of his job.

But General Anastacio Bustamante, Northwest Commandant, was cut from different cloth, for he controlled a large body of troops and could measure swords with anybody. Though concerned about armed filibusters from the United States who would seize Texas and set up an independent state, he was pleased with Steve's plans for orderly settlement. He felt that Texas should be developed rapidly.

Steve rode on south much encouraged.

Waters had dropped off in Monterrey. The short rest there had done Andrews worlds of good, but he tired badly while traveling across the desolate country to Saltillo. When told that the city needed a physician, Andrews decided to stay on with friends.

Steve had to journey on alone. To avoid being attacked, he dressed in ragged peon clothes. Dust swirled over in clouds. He grew more and more discouraged.

San Luis Potosí was badly decayed. Its rich conquest mines had been idle for a century and a half, but the cathedral, government houses, and fine residences, which circled the gardenlike alameda, were impressive. Yet Steve was disturbed by the ignorance and superstition that thrived in the shadow of the finest palaces.

That night the plaza music floated under the sharp stars, and folk promenaded in their finery. The balmy night filled him with vague longings. He thought of Eliza but mostly about the difficulties of his mission. If he failed, disaster would strike hundreds of settlers on the move to his grant.

3

It was April 29, at daybreak, that Steve emerged from the lofty mountains above Mexico City. He reined in his horse to look over the colossal, breath-taking panorama.

Vivid was the contrast with the region he had just come

through. Here really was a "Garden of Eden." As though cupped in the hands of God, in the circle of mighty mountains, the enormous city and its populous suburbs stretched out for miles among gardens and trees to extinct volcanic cones. The golden towers and domes of this city of palaces poked up beside dazzling silver lakes. Above this stupendous spectacle soared the mighty snow volcanoes Popocatepetl and Iztaccihuatl—the "Smoke Mountain" and the "White Woman"—dazzling in the clear, upland morning air. By late afternoon the lofty white slopes turned rose and violet with flashes of gold from perpetual glaciers—a glory and splendor forever.

Steve was coming into this vast alien city, knowing nobody except Baron de Bastrop. He scarcely spoke the language. He was ignorant "of the laws, the forms, the customs, the disposition and feelings of the new Government" —an utter stranger in a place that until two years before had wholly forebade foreigners. They were "proscribed by the Laws and Discountenanced by the people." He was bound to meet suspicion and hostility. In his pocket he had barely enough money to get along for a few months, let alone for the successful prosecution of his business. To make matters worse, he learned that Baron de Bastrop had returned to Texas.

4

Mexico City was larger, richer, more impressive than even New York, and Steve never tired of reiterating his admiration for its elegance and beauty. He spent much time in seeing its sights. He was attracted by the bright shops and crowded markets, the neighborhood Indian dances, and the gaudy military parades. They gave the city a theatrical quality. At the opera, where a box cost $500 a season, and at the lavish official *Te Deums* in the cathedral, celebrated with all the pomp and ceremony revered by the Latin mind, richly dressed folk and officers wearing gaudy uniforms and silver swords made a gallant show.

Nearly half of General Iturbide's decorative army was made up of officers, noncoms, and musicians—in bright red-and-blue uniforms—with waving pennants and velvet-embroidered standards, stripes and bars and braid. The dictator constantly paraded his new mounted palace guards, resplendent in purple and scarlet plumage, to the fanfare of bellowing bugles, pounding drums, and cannon fire.

But Steve also saw the misery of the poor *pelados*. "The population . . . is very . . . mixed . . . a great proportion . . . miserably poor and wretched, beggars . . . more numerous than I ever saw in any place." Robberies and assassinations were frequent. The people were extremely "bigoted and superstitious." Indolence appeared to be "the general order of the day."

Steve soon made friends in high places. Prospects for getting his land grant validated seemed bright. Congress was already working on a colonization law. He wrote Hawkins optimistically that he expected to finish in ten or twelve days. "General Iturbide seems to have the happiness of his country much at heart, and I have no doubt he will act as a great and good man ought to."

6 · Hail the Emperor

"TOMORROW YOU MUST PRESENT your case to the Committee on Colonization," Congressman Lorenzo de Zavala told Steve.

They were sitting in the black-leather lounge of the Chamber of Deputies. Chubby small Lorenzo was an eternal dynamo.

"We shall get your petition to the floor of Congress by the middle of the month," he promised, "but you must talk to the committee members personally. They do not know Texas, and all sorts of scoundrels are trying to get grants."

The city buzzed with American and European adventurers who were trying to obtain trade concessions or land and mining grants in Texas and elsewhere to get the jump on everybody else by snatching rich plums from the hard-

40

pressed new government. Several shady Europeans wanted to settle large numbers of Germans and Irish.

"General Arthur G. Wavell," continued Don Lorenzo, smoothing back his dark hair, "is seeking a land grant in the Galveston area. He has great influence, for he has just been made a colonel of the Mexican army out of gratitude for his help to the Chileans in their struggle for freedom. But no claim is as valid as yours. It would be a disgrace not to recognize it."

General James Wilkinson also was asking for Texas land. He had headed the American forces that had taken over Louisiana from France, and stories about him were confused. One tale implicated him in Aaron Burr's plot to set up an independent nation in the Southwest.

"He came with a letter to me," Stephen told Zavala.

"Go easy. Some believe he is a secret agent of the United States government, working on a plot to steal part of Mexico."

"Robert Leftwich wants land north of my colony," said Steve. "That would relieve my people from attacks by Comanches, so I hope his petition is favorably received."

"We'll see," suggested Zavala. "We Mexicans should set up our own colonies alongside American settlements."

Stephen was not sure that he agreed. Before going before the committee, he received the disquieting news that General Trespalacios—the exiled independence officer with whom he had had a tiff in New Orleans for his aid to filibusters—had replaced Governor Martínez. The changeover jeopardized all his efforts. A letter from Joe Hawkins confirmed his worst fears.

On Trespalacios' staff were former filibusters who

wanted an independent Texas and hated Steve. Two of them and Colonel Benjamin Milam, a fire-eating Kentuckian, had asked for land grants. It would require cleverness to block them. Quick action was necessary.

Further, not all members of Zavala's colonization committee were friendly to Steve. Several were downright hostile. One, Zavala had warned him, had been bought off by promises of land from the Europeans. All of them feared the United States because of the armed filibuster attacks on Texas ever since 1811.

Steve assured them of his own loyalty to Mexico and the value of his settlement to the country. His great knowledge of Texas won their respect, but few believed that such a vast wilderness could be tamed without troops to hold back the Indians.

Steve reported that preseverance and industry, the ax, the plow, and the hoe would do more than rifle or sword. "Freemen can defend themselves," he insisted.

After the session about the big mahogany table, Zavala assured him that the majority would support his claim. "You were very convincing," he added.

Most enthusiastic had been Congressman Juan Bautista Arizpe from Monterrey. He knew the north country, and his opinion carried weight. His brother, a prominent Puebla churchman, was also high in Republican politics.

Steve promised Arizpe land in his colony and told him of his project for controlling Indian trade. Arizpe suggested that he send an outline of his plan to General Bustamante. The good will of the commandant in the north was all important.

Steve worked out a draft of his plan. He could be helpful "by inducing merchants in the United States to take stock." He put in a strong plug for his colony. The Indians were giving Bustamante increasing trouble, and the settlement would provide a strong bulwark.

2

Steve's petition was put on the calendar for floor debate on March 18, 1822.

It was an unfortunate moment. The conflict between Congress and Iturbide broke wide open that day. Bent on economy and fearing Iturbide's power, Congress had drastically slashed army salaries and appropriations. Bitterness between "the Liberator" and "the free sovereign Congress" came head on. Iturbide resigned. Friends and enemies were thrown into consternation, and Congress broke up in wild shouting and fist fights.

That night a mysterious Sergeant Pío Marcha assembled the officers and soldiers of one of Iturbide's regiments at the San Hipólito barracks. Tossing out handfuls of money, he led them as armed gangs through the streets. Stirred up by these paid agents, the mobs grew to fantastic size. All night the city blazed with light. All night the church bells rang out, a roll of never-ending sound across the flat roofs. Members of Congress who opposed Iturbide were yanked out of bed by the soldiers and dragged off to prison. The general was determined to impose his will on Congress and the nation. His pious resignation had been a fraud to overthrow the republic.

On Sunday, at the unusual hour of seven, all members of Congress not in hiding or in jail assembled at the Congress building under stern orders to ratify Iturbide's seizure of power and his elevation to imperial rule as Emperor Agustín I.

3

The colonization bill finally was passed on November 27 and was sent to the emperor for his signature. It authorized such land grants as Austin's.

Steve wrote Andrews gaily that he intended to spend Christmas with him in Saltillo. His joy over the passing of the colonization bill had been enhanced by the knowledge that Lovelace was safe. The *Lively,* driven by bad storms, had landed its settlers and provisions at the mouth of the Brazos.

But this was not a lasting comfort to Steve. The new year brought fresh trouble. Generals Nicolás Bravo and Vicente Guerrero openly declared "for the restoration of the rights of Liberty of the Nation." They had a big following and controlled much of the regular army. Further, General Antonio López de Santa Anna led his crack Eighth Cavalry Regiment through surging Veracruz crowds to go forth to seize the capital. Like Iturbide, Santa Anna was a gaudy military show-off, addicted to cockfights, morphine, and gambling, but he had boundless energy, cunning, and ambition. He struck the gong of unrest loudly and was joined by popular General Guadalupe Victoria.

4

However, the emperor finally signed the colonization law on January 4, 1823. Jubilantly Steve wrote the good news to Governor Trespalacios.

But he had maintained "a uniform patient smiling countenance" for so long that his bottled-up bitterness also poured forth.

The past winter . . . I suffered everything a man could suffer in a desert without provisions and exposed . . . to the inclemency of the season and ferocious Indians. . . . I have endured all the mortifications, evils and unpleasant setbacks . . . which fall upon all those who have the misfortune to find themselves dependent upon the Government in this Court. . . . The vexations . . . this law has cost me are indescribable.

Even now such clauses "could be improved," but before he would ask anything more, "however simple," he "would abandon in desperation all idea of establishing himself in the Empire." They should "give thanks to heaven" for any law at all.

Not till January 18 did Iturbide—by then fighting for his life—find a breathing spell to sign the Austin decree. Unfortunately, it was vague about Steve's authority and his right to found towns. He wanted all conditions in black and white.

But Iturbide had to rush off to Puebla, a city that had just risen against him. Rocking on his throne, the emperor had to eat crow and call the legal Congress back into session. Only those in the Junta risked attending.

Amid this mounting confusion, Steve wrote the Minister of Relations that he had been waiting here since April and was still waiting eleven months later. His colony was well-nigh ruined by long uncertainty, bad crops, and Indian attacks.

To his surprise the official signed the amendments to the decree the very next day, March 11.

By then the revolutionists were closing in relentlessly. This promised fresh headaches for Steve. Would the emperor's land grant hold water with the new crowd? Would the endless rigmarole have to be faced again?

Friends and lawyers advised him to clinch the matter with the new regime. As he could not get back to Texas through the flame of revolt, he stayed on, watching the swift bloody drama unfold, until Iturbide abdicated on March 19 and departed for exile in Italy.

7 · Clearing the Wilderness

AFTER LEAVING MEXICO CITY, Stephen was held up for three months in Monterrey to iron out the details as to how his grant would be managed.

Bustamante had been replaced by General Felipe de la Garza, who was Steve's friend. After two months of consultation with the legislature, Garza ruled that Austin had supreme judicial power except in cases involving the death penalty and lawsuits concerning more than a few hundred dollars. Serious offenders were to be held at hard labor until their fate could be decided by superior authorities. Stephen was given the rank of lieutenant colonel and authorized to organize a militia battalion.

Another month went by before the governor appointed a land commissioner. To Steve's delight Baron de Bastrop was chosen. Steve went on to San Antonio for a joyous reunion with James, Erasmo Seguín, and Juan Martín de Veramendi.

Governor Trespalacios offered every assistance and lavish entertainment. But Steve and Bastrop hurried on to Sylvanius Castleman's ranch on the Colorado.

A tall genial man with tufted eyebrows, Castleman stamped out in big boots. "The very man we're waiting for!" he shouted. "And the good baron, too! Are we going to kill the fatted calf! Fortunately the pesky Indians left us a few beeves."

Mrs. Castleman, a lively buxom woman with four children, had the servants on the fly, and the two guests sat down to a bountiful meal of spareribs, dumplings, and pumpkin pie.

Castleman insisted that Austin and Bastrop make his big log cabin their headquarters till a town could be laid out.

Bastrop issued a proclamation that, as militia head, Austin had "full powers to administer justice and preserve good order." All unsuccessful applicants for colony land who did not move "further into the interior," would be expelled by force.

In a message from "the Colorado house of Mr. Castleman," Steve reported on what he had accomplished in Mexico City and explained that titles signed by him and Bastrop would be perfect "forever." The land could be sold, traded, and mortgaged, just like property in the United States. Steve called for militia volunteers, whom he agreed to pay out of his own pocket. Settlers who caused disorder would meet with stern treatment. They must "have confidence" in him and "be directed" by him. He felt the

"same interest in their prosperity" as for his "own family.
. . . Let us be united as one man."

Steve had his hands full every minute. Bell's preliminary
land allotments had brought discord. It was not easy to
please everybody. The tract Stephen had chosen for himself on the Colorado had been occupied. Even his good assistant Bell and another settler wanted Stephen's other reserve on the Brazos.

Stephen reminded Bell of his Colorado River loss. He
had picked the Brazos tract to have "a place at the bottom
of the prairie to live at." But he added generously, "If it
had not been for you . . . the whole settlement would
have been broken. . . . I am not difficult to please nor
avaricious, and will sacrifice my own interests at any time
in favor of those I esteem or wish to serve." Before he
would "take an inch of that place," he would "drink river
water. Occupy what you want without interference from
anyone. Just select some other tract for me," he added.
"I'm too busy settling disputes, pushing surveying, tend-
ing to financial matters and records, and granting titles to
choose it for myself."

He had to issue navigation permits, name militia officers, and arrange for militia elections. A town had to be
laid out. A torrent of letters from would-be settlers had to
be answered, and new arrivals had to be examined in person. He had to keep a detailed record of all money and
goods paid in.

The account of Jared E. Groce, who was to become the
richest planter in the colony, showed that he had put up
for his land $326.49—$100 cash, another $100 in notes,

the rest in merchandise: "linin, lining, buttons," black and colored cotton and silk thread, a vest pattern, and so on. The cloth was valued from $3.50 to $10 a yard. Two black silk handkerchiefs came to $4.

On his side Stephen hired three Negro slaves from Groce —a woman at eight dollars a month and two men at fifteen—"said Negroes . . . to be well-treated by me . . . the said Groce . . . to clothe them. Should they run away or die the loss is to be Groce's—sickness . . . my loss."

2

Though Steve was performing every sort of duty and was scarcely meeting expenses and had received nothing for the two years of exploration or for the long battle in Mexico City and Monterrey, settlers murmured bitterly about the required payment of 12½ cents an acre. Malcontents grumbled that Austin would get $75,000 for settling the first 150 colonists. But even should he receive such an amount, it would scarcely cover expenses.

He called a meeting to remind the settlers of all he had been through. To get a few dollars with which to start, he had signed away much of the land he would receive personally as manager of the grant. He had the legal right, before granting any title, to receive the "bit," or 12½ cents an acre, in cash and in full. But when hardship existed, he would wait two, three, or more years. He did have to have some hard money to pay to surveyors and to the government, but otherwise he would take horses, mules, cattle, hogs, poultry, furs, beeswax, honey, homemade cloth, and dressed deerskins.

He priced such things generously above market value, though often they resulted in a dead loss.

To Bell, Stephen said sharply, "I have risked my life, my health, my property, my all in this enterprise. Those who complain without reason may have cause to regret it."

Almost the only one who knew Spanish, Steve had to carry on voluminous correspondence with the Mexican civil and military authorities in San Antonio, Saltillo, and Mexico City. Federal, state, and local governments asked him for numerous reports, which often required endless investigation but for which he was paid nothing: a survey of Galveston Harbor, maps, information on rival land petitions, immigrant Indians from the United States, fauna, and flora. He was even asked for specimens.

Orders, not always reasonable, came from San Antonio, now ruled not by a governor but by a political chief. Trespalacios had been ousted, charged with graft and crimes against the state. Among those defrauded had been Littleberry Hawkins, who had gone back to Kentucky after losing everything. The new chief, José Antonio Saucedo, though not always aware of the trouble that some of his regulations caused, backed up Austin firmly, warning unruly elements that the colonel's authority was absolute.

Other instructions came from Saltillo, the new capital of the combined state of Coahuila and Texas. When a serious food shortage developed, the governor asked Steve to send him chickens and pigs. His old friend Arizpe, writing from Monterrey about politics, added the usual postscript. "If you visit New Orleans please order me ten yards of light-weave cloth of Popotilla, and a muskrat cap, the skins of which are so plentiful there." Seguín wanted him to buy a phaeton. Saucedo wanted a strong cot and low-heeled shoes. Señora María Josefa Augustina Bezerri, of San Antonio, wrote that James had promised her two roosters and a hatchet. Later, when Bastrop went off to serve in the state legislature, his first letter closed with the request, "Don't neglect to send me powder, tobacco, blue cloth for the Indians, Vermillion and the other things I asked for . . . and don't forget a horse with a good gait." Bastrop's successor at San Felipe demanded that Steve send a carriage for him and his family to Saltillo—nearly 1,000 miles distant.

Colonists asked him to settle quarrels, write letters and contracts, collect or assume debts, cash drafts, block claims for old debts in the United States, and trace lost persons and property. Often he was asked to buy tobacco or other things on only vague promises of future payment.

Steve's many tasks demanded day-and-night attention, wise decisions, tact, and self-reliance. His duties were never finished.

3

In spite of careful scanning of references, lawless elements slipped in—the famous GTTs, "Gone to Texas to escape the law." One stock greeting was, "What did you run away from back East?" If a man denied anything wrong, he was suspected of not being a man or of having done something really dreadful. Steve found numbers of malefactors to punish, thieves to track down, and lost horses and cattle to be recovered.

To Bell on the Brazos, he wrote pointedly:

I rely greatly on your prudence and judgment in preserving harmony. . . . [Those not worthy] must be ordered off. . . . Examine Red River emigrants very closely and take care no bad men get in—let us have no black sheep in our flock. Should a man of notorious bad character come in, I . . . authorize you to whip him not exceeding fifty lashes and seize sufficient of his property to pay a guard to conduct him beyond the Trinity River. One example of this kind is wanting badly and after that we shall not be troubled . . . shall treat the settlers as my children and Brothers but shall exercise that firmness and energy which my duty to the government of my adoption, to the common good of the Colony, and to my own family require.

Steve ordered one evil character whipped back to Nacogdoches and obliged five men and their families to leave posthaste. Several were murderers with rewards on their heads. One drunken acquaintance was wanted for counterfeiting.

Indian affairs consumed time and money. Steve's policy was conciliatory and he overlooked minor offenses, for many farms were too remote to be protected. The settlers needed peace and security, and until the colony was strongly established, he sought to remain on good terms. If bloodshed could be avoided, in time new settlers to the north would fend off the Indians.

He had to entertain many visiting chiefs and provide them and their scores of followers with presents and food from his own pocket. Besides the cost this took time and patience.

Friendly tactics did not ward off all trouble. With thirty men he marched against the Karankawa who had stolen valuable horses and cattle on the Brazos and obliged Chief Carita to surrender all stolen animals and flog the guilty braves with his own hand. Next time, Steve warned, the culprits would be shot.

He pressed the military authorities to pay the militia and assist in defense. Finding that his letters to the latest Saltillo commandant brought little result, Stephen went over his head to the Mexican War Department to ask that men be added to the militia that guarded the colony's northern frontier. For months the militia had received no pay. Powder sent them was too coarse-grained for the carbines. He also wished to add ten more mounted men and a sergeant to protect travelers. Bandits and Indians made all roads dangerous. "This evil will increase . . . if . . . not scotched at once." No answer came.

But Minister of State Lucas Alamán, a clerical reactionary acting as head of the cabinet for the triumvirate of "liberal republican generals," forebade all public assemblages and denied local authorities the right of petition. When the colonists came to exercise constitutional rights, such restrictions would provoke resistance.

Steve wrote back blandly, placing his colony under Alamán's protection. He had labored "faithfully for near three years in these unsettled wilds exposed to every danger and hardship and fatigue." The colonists, enduring so many privations, were still threatened with famine resulting from drought. They were exposed to attacks by hostile Indians and pilfering by tribes professing to be friendly. An efficient police was needed to punish "fugitives and vagabonds from both nations." Having no jail or troops to hold prisoners, he had had to permit criminals to go unpunished or inflict corporal punishment.

I need not comment [he concluded] on the great benefits which will result to this Province from holding back hostile Indians, providing resources to support the government, and furnishing Agriculturists and Mechanics to bring into use the riches of this heretofore uninhabited portion of the great Mexican Nation. The wisdom of your Excellency will discover all these things.

4

Steve hastened to lay out and build the new capital town, already officially designated San Felipe de Austin. He chose a Brazos River site on the land of a settler who was recompensed with a lifelong ferry concession.

Stephen and Seth Ingram halted their horses on the high river bluff. "A magnificent spot!" exclaimed Stephen, looking fondly at the timber. "What kind of trees do we have?"

Ingram rattled off the list, "Live oak, black oak, red oak, post oak, white oak, pecan, ash, cottonwood. . . ."

"And as I live, mulberries already purple ripe. . . ."

"The underbrush is wild peach and sassafras—kind of a nuisance to grub out."

"The Indians make tea from the bark to thin the blood at springtime."

"I can put a road down that gully to the river," suggested Seth, pointing to little Palmito Creek.

"Fine! And back there on the creek about a half mile is where I want my house."

"I'll fix up just below you," said Seth.

"It's ideal hereabouts for farming and stock raising—

plenty of good range. Those canebrake bottoms on the other shore are fine for corn. What we need in and about our new capital are plenty of decent families, men of judgment, no riffraff, good sound citizens."

They rode back into the prairie. "The very spot for the plaza!"

"Better tell me just how you want things laid out," suggested Seth.

"How about a drive along the river bluff, say 20 feet wide, and a central street, maybe 12 vara [about 35 feet] wide? Make as many farms as you can front on the river."

"How big do you want the plaza?"

Steve rode along slowly, gesturing. "We'll set aside the center lot for the *palacio*, or town hall. Someday, there opposite, we'll have a church."

Among those who looked in on them was Bill Dewees, now settled on the Colorado. He wanted to see how the new town was getting along. But he had to race home because Indians were reported attacking lone women in a ranch house. The supposed marauders turned out to be friendly berrypickers.

Steve wrote Bell that he could select any lot in town that he wanted and chided him for his poor farming methods. Good prairie peach land should not be used for corn, which grew best in fertile watered cane bottoms. He apologized for his bluntness. His good friend Joe Hawkins had just died in New Orleans; and with so many things to vex him, his friends should bear with his occasional shortness of temper.

Steve threw up a stout log cabin on Palmito Creek. It had a central open hall and two chimneys in the wings.

Here in his log-cabin capitol, Stephen issued his first proclamation from San Felipe de Austin, December 2, 1823, "the third year of Independence and the second year of Liberty of the Mexican nation."

8 · Building the Edifice

ON MAY 1, 1824, STEVE looked out at the golden bloom of the gnarled huisache trees on the Constitutional Plaza of his new town of San Felipe de Austin. A crowd in Sunday best was gathered to celebrate the new Mexican constitution. A five-piece band was playing on the porch of Peyton's tavern, and men were tacking up green-white-and-red Mexican flags.

Planned as a Spanish-American settlement, already San Felipe bore the stamp of frontier America that was not Spanish. Rather than clustering about the plaza, it preferred to straggle—along one road beside Palmito Creek and the river—like little boom towns everywhere in the American West. As the local gunsmith, Noah Smithwick, remarked, it was "like Samantha Allen's funeral procession: pretty good as to length but rather thin."

The store fronts had ugly, bare false-board foreheads

like those along the main streets of all mid-America. The houses were not thatched or flat adobe as in La Bahía and San Antonio; they were whole-log cabins, with slanting clapboard roofs, resembling those scattered through Kentucky and Missouri.

As yet San Felipe had no church and no public buildings. Steve's cabin still served as office, inn, and town hall. In Mexican towns the administrative building was always the "palace," however humble. But for Austin's colonists, were it ever built, it would be a plain, old-fashioned town hall where folk would meet for elections and discussions and where deeds and births and marriages would be recorded.

Official records in Stephen's office were in both Spanish and English, but all settler petitions were in English— that scrawled, misspelled, half-illiterate English of the frontier dawn, a living echo of colloquial Americanisms of the wilderness: Mississippi drawl; Ozark tang; twisted, throaty South Indiana accent; Yankee nasal "ers"; the soft music of the New Orleans Delta; and the broad vowels of Virginia.

The mayor was called an alcalde according to Mexican law, but the clerk who sent out the first election notice, unable to spell that "heathen" word, wrote "alcaldy."

Now the people were assembling to take the oath of allegiance to the new Mexican constitution, but not one in two score could even read it.

Steve had written Political Chief Saucedo that he had set this day, May 1, to promulgate the new national magna charta with "all the solemnity and enthusiasm required by that important and glorious subject."

And so, on this particularly sunny May day, Stephen Fuller Austin, lieutenant colonel of the Mexican army and political chief with unlimited powers over the Colorado and the Brazos, looked out over the crowd and thought of the road that Mexico and his colony had traveled since the downfall of Iturbide.

He was pleased with the turn that national affairs had taken. Earlier he had been a strong advocate of the imperial system. Observation and experience, however, had taught him much. The abuses of Iturbide's unrestricted power had made him value the duties and liberties of free government.

Dictatorial reaction had been held at bay, and the new federal constitution of 1824, to which Steve had contributed so much, had been adopted. It was one of the enlightened documents of the century and far superior to prevailing arbitrary systems in most of the world at that time. Like his colony, the Mexican nation was being built anew. The walls harbored the freedom he wished for his own people.

Steve stepped upon the special flag-draped platform to face the crowd of weather-beaten settlers.

Fellow citizens, . . . I am convinced that there is not a breast amongst you that will not palpitate with exultation and delight at the prospects of freedom, happiness, and prosperity which the federal republican system of government presents to your view. . . . The great Mexican nation is free. Rational liberty with all its concomitant blessings has opened to the view of the world a nation which despotism had hitherto enveloped in intellectual night. . . . The hitherto enslaved Spanish provinces are now free and independent states.

2

Already Texas had elected representatives to the state legislature in Saltillo and to the federal Congress. Both were happy choices—Baron de Bastrop and Erasmo Seguín.

Steve wrote them about the desires of the colonists. He urged Bastrop to see that a local recorder's office was set up, that a priest was sent, and that no sudden drastic anti-slavery legislation was passed.

To Seguín he wrote that the two problems of immigration were slavery and religion. Catholics from Louisiana would not immigrate unless they could bring their slaves. From states with few Catholics, not many would come if there was "no liberty of conscience."

Seguín replied in his usual terse way that Texas had always practiced religious tolerance. He abhorred slavery, but Texan-Americans had been granted special rights, so they should have at least temporary guarantees. If the region was to be developed rapidly, the labor problem had to be solved.

In spite of Seguín's efforts, a federal decree of July 13, 1824, prohibited traffic in slaves forever. They were freed by the mere fact of setting foot on Mexican soil. Children of resident slaves were also freed.

The slaveholding colonists assembled in San Felipe and protested wrathfully. Steve calmed them down. Although the new law prevented the bringing of slaves to Texas, the existing situation was not greatly disturbed.

Seguín reported that the government planned to send

north 800 or 1,000 "vagabonds"—unfortunately, people not used to working—"not much good." It was also planned to send up 6,000 Mexican settlers in October. Neither plan was carried through.

Startling news came through that Itúrbide had landed on the coast of Tamaulipas. He was quickly captured by Felipe de la Garza and put before a firing squad in the town of Padilla on July 19, 1824, exactly a year after he had abdicated.

The new government seemed firmer than ever, and Steve paused to take full stock of his colony. The last of the 300 settlers were moving in. Nearly all the colony land was allotted. Surveys were made and deeds were filed. Cabins had been built; there were even a few good houses of wood or brick. Roads had been cut through, and ferries had been installed. Crops were in. Corn leaped tasseled and fair from the cane bottoms. Cotton—first tried out by Jared E. Groce 20 miles above San Felipe—was bursting with white boles and promised to become a bonanza product. Tobacco, too, would be a profitable crop if settlers' petitions for permission to grow it were ever heeded, for the government bought large quantities to give to the Indians to keep them pacified.

Livestock was multiplying. Babies were being born. Since there was no priest yet, Steve had recently officiated at the first wedding.

The outlook was bright. The groundwork had been laid; the walls were up. Now the roof was going on. The colony was almost built.

Peace and civilized habits were gaining ground. Though the western tide of settlement in the United States continued to push unruly Indians into Texas, settlers beyond San Felipe bore the brunt, and within a few years Steve was able to boast that every family was secure in life and property. The settlers by then did not even have bolts on their doors or locks on their stables.

Only one case of burglary was ever reported. For a long time it was a simple, friendly society. The people ate plain food and lived in plain houses; nobody was rich and nobody was poor. If many tasks still remained, at least he and his colonists had found reasonable security and growing prosperity.

On a desk pad, as he sat by the window looking down Palmito Creek, he jotted down the principles that had guided him: "The redemption of Texas from the wilderness, fidelity and gratitude to my adopted country, inflexibly true to the interests and just rights of my settlers."

He had come to save his family and gain personal fortune, but the task of building up the colony had absorbed all his effort and thought. To that he had subordinated all his own ease and private interests. Personally, he had little to show for his sacrifice. "A moneyed fanatic would say I have followed a shadow." The hardest was now over. "The few clouds that still hang over us are mere shadows compared to those gone by."

Down the winding gully he could see the little ferry taking a drove of cattle across the Brazos River. Here, less than three years before, had been the haunt of buffalo and deer. Brazos de Dios was the full name of the stream—"Arms of God." His new town rested in the arms of God, and Stephen himself rested in the arms of God—so it seemed after all the trials and tribulations.

3

Steve decided to bring his entire family to Texas. Shortly after he had reached Mexico City, Bryan died, leaving Emily widowed with four children and heavy debts, which Steve had shouldered. When Austin got back to Texas—without a cent and his clothing worn out—he was driven "nearly mad," as he wrote his sister, that he could not aid them. Thrilled that at last he could draw his family together again, he took pen in hand to write them to come.

He still had misgivings. He was almost without money and bowed down with debts. All he had was a part share in the 63,000 premium acres, which were not yet productive.

Would his family be happy here? Conditions were still primitive. Could Maria, whose health had been poor since Moses' death, stand the long hard trip? Steve had to warn her and Emily bluntly just what to expect.

We have all had good Schooling in the best School in the World . . . Adversity. . . . Our prospects . . . are beginning to look up, but we must . . . remember our past troubles . . . not forget . . . wealth is hard to acquire and easily lost—let our motto therefore be economy and plain living.

He dipped his pen in the bowl of shot and wiped it clean.

To set an example to the rest of the settlers, it is my wish nothing be worn in the family but homespun for several years. . . . Everything about the house should be plain and pretty much like the rest of my neighbors—we are all poor in this country and therefore all on an equality. As long as this continues there will be harmony and good-neighborship. You know how easy it is to give offense to a certain class of mankind. Because of my position all the acts of my family will be watched. Uniform affable deportment is required of all of you.

He wished her to bring in Bryan's slaves, the widow Sarah and her five children, as "contract" workers. If Aunt Austin, Maria's sister, who had a large family, would dispose of everything in Missouri, he would give her free his "Spring tract East of the Colorado," between the river, a creek, and the prairie, and would lend her all the corn she needed for the first year; he would do everything in his "power to aid her."

The sea route from New Orleans would be shortest, cheapest, and, barring bad winds, the easiest, but the overland route, if more fatiguing, was preferable provided several families would join. Horses should be sent overland to Natchitoches, and the wagons, carts, and other property should be brought on a keelboat, which could be sold for as much as it cost.

"You must not bring much of anything except beds and bedding and castings [iron pots] and crockery ware for House use." Maria's piano should be shipped to New Orleans to come by water, or he would buy a new one later on. All other heavy objects and furniture should be sold to get money for "pork, flour, Beans, etc." . . . enough provisions "to last the whole journey. . . . Bring a pair of geese and tame ducks—also all kind of garden seeds . . . Cabbage, Lettuce, beets, Sages, Summer Savory, horse-radish, etc. and at Natchez or lower down, try and get some orange, fig and grape roots." Have "brother get some Nectarine and peach Stones . . . and a dozen young Pears or the seeds of his best Pears and apples, also some crab apple seeds. I want them to try to make a hedge, also the cypress vine or any other vine for an arbor, and some roots of the double Rose, all these can be brought in a small box and watered. . . ."

Have some "good Bacon and Pickled Pork and beef dried and pickled"; also bring from Missouri "several barrels of beans or peas and hominy, etc. for the journey, also dried apples and peaches." All such things, as well as "Homemade Linsey or Cotton cloth or tow or flax linin," sell high in "Nackitosh" and in Texas. At Alexandria or "Natches" they should lay in a good supply of sugar, coffee, tea, spices, and rice. "Bring a steel mill . . . will cost about 12 dollars. . . . Bring tools." A large tent was necessary.

They were to bring all the books they could "to pass away the time." But be "as saving of every cent as possible."

To his sister he inserted a special note. "Be careful of mother and let us try to meet once more in this world and perhaps this mild climate may preserve her precious life to us many years."

Now Steve felt it was high time to pick a wife. Eliza was married. A friend wrote that, if Steve would come to Missouri, he could "pick . . . off" a very desirable girl just widowed. His mother reminded him of a girl in New Orleans he had liked.

Steve asked a land promoter he had met in Mexico to find out if a Miss Williams, of Columbia, Mississippi, whom he had known in college days and who was now widowed, would be interested in living in Texas. His friend reported that she was wide-eyed at the query.

His brother James was to leave to bring Maria, Emily, and the others to Texas, and Steve asked him to call on old friends in Natchitoches, particularly Sibley. "Send two reams of good writing paper for deeds . . . a large blank book . . . 2 yards of Red buntin or flannel 2 of Green and 2 of White for a flag, some narrow Red, White and Green ribbon for cockades." James was also to bring shoes for all and "barks and Salts . . . a good Mosquitoe bar."

The last item Stephen underlined as he viciously slapped at his temple.

James must not spend a cent more than he had to and was to try to salvage the tangled remnants of their ill-starred business efforts in Little Rock. He was to encourage "all good, moral and industrious men of families . . . to move out to Texas"; for Steve had been granted permission to settle 500 additional families—maybe 800.

James was to buy three more slaves. When the group was ready, Stephen would send horses and mules to Louisiana to be sold so that they could buy "a few cows . . . to . . . give milk on the road."

But when James reached Natchitoches on May 23, he found a letter that told him of Maria's death. He went on sadly to Hazel Run. There on July 18 Maria's sister had also died, leaving "a large and helpless Family of Children. God only knows what is to become of them!" James still planned to bring back Emily and her children, but she married James Perry, a storekeeper near the lead mines.

Steve's friend in Mississippi wrote that "the fair one . . . to wit, Miss Williams," indulged the hope of seeing Steve in the spring. "You will not regret your visit to her. . . ." But the bitterness of death and heavy new duties drove all thought of marriage out of Steve's head. He was carrying on to full success, but all his intimate hopes and emotions had been defrauded.

9 · Revolt on the Sabine

THE TOWNSPEOPLE OF SAN FELIPE stood at their doors that
gray January day of 1827 and watched Mexican troops
file wearily into the plaza on their wiry cayuses, rifles
strapped to their saddles. At their head, under a big hat,
rode Colonel Mateo Ahumada, Military Commandant, and
Don José Antonio Saucedo, Political Chief of Texas, in a
leather ranchero suit. Alongside were Stephen Austin and
the local alcalde, John P. Coles. They had traveled out to
welcome the forces.

Things had grown serious in East Texas that Christmas
and New Year's. Reckless men on the Sabine frontier were
riding wild. Several minor fracases had grown into open
revolt. The free Republic of Fredonia had been declared.
Now Mexican troops were on the move to put it down.

The new frontier republic was the handiwork of a few

bold American settlers, desperadoes, and former filibusters. An ill-tempered *empresario,* Haden Edwards, and his brother spearheaded the trouble.

Two years before, Haden had been given a big grant east of Austin's colony. Soon he created an ugly rift between Americans and old-time Mexican families, whose land he tried to seize. Time and again the government sternly rebuked him. Now his new Fredonian government had called upon the Indians to take back their lost hunting grounds all the way from the Red River to the Rio Grande. The tough Red River men at Pecan Point and the Austin settlers were invited to support the newborn nation.

Austin and his colony had shown steadfast loyalty to Mexico. But would the rallying cry of fellow Americans prove stronger? How many Austinites would respond to the Fredonian call? What would be Stephen Austin's stand? How far would revolt spread?

Ahumada and Saucedo had approached the Austin settlement with great caution. As the troops crossed the Guadalupe and moved through American farms along the Colorado and the Brazos, both officials were astonished at the snug log cabins, the long stretches of corn and cotton, the large herds of pigs and cows and horses, all the industry and prosperity. Nowhere did they encounter hostility or see signs of unrest.

As they led their troops into San Felipe, a big Mexican flag, with its eagle on a cactus, hung from Stephen's house, which still served as the town hall. Smaller green-white-and-red flags had been tacked up among now-wilted Christmas boughs on the tavern run by Mr. and Mrs. Jonathan C. Peyton, the Cooper and Chieves grogshop and billiard hall, the stores of Dinsmore and White, and the new story-and-a-half Whiteside Hotel.

In his house, over brandy, Steve told Ahumada and Saucedo, "I tried my best to settle this foolishness peacefully. I sent word to the troublemakers that there was only one way they could save themselves: Present themselves immediately to you in person and admit without any stiff, foolish Republican obstinacy that they had taken wrong steps."

From his desk Stephen pulled out a copy of his letter. "Here are the very words: 'Let the Americans put aside their rifles and be guided by . . . prudence and reason.' Let them 'be obedient to the laws and seek redress only in the legal mode.' "

"Now it is serious," put in Ahumada, shifting his double cartridge belt, crisscrossed over shoulders and chest. He was a big lean man, slim as a tiger.

With a clang of big-roweled, diamond-blue spurs, Ahumada left to see that his troops camped in the rain on the river bluffs were comfortable. The horses had been loosed to graze on the river bottom, and the soldiers were trying to cook meat and toast *tortillas* over hissing fires. Stephen had ordered steers slaughtered.

Shortly before the revolt a Mexican officer, General Manuel de Mier y Terán, had come through East Texas to investigate stories of unrest and plots. He called on Steve in San Felipe and went on to the frontier.

He found the border population a strange mixture. Armed Indians were ready for war. Colonists "of another people," more aggressive and better informed than the

Mexican inhabitants, were "shrewd and unruly." The frontier Mexicans, mostly "poor and ignorant," and the "venal and corrupt" Mexican officials were "despised" by the outlanders.

Among the latter, besides "honest laborers," were "fugitives from justice . . . vagabonds and criminals," some of whom Austin had whipped out of his colony. But "honorable and dishonorable alike" were demanding "the privileges and authority and offices" which the constitution guaranteed. Slaves, learning of "the favorable interest" that the Mexican law took toward their condition, were asking for freedom.

A land rush had added to the problem. Floods in Mississippi and Louisiana had driven people across the Sabine. Austin's great success had encouraged hundreds to head for Texas. The restlessness of the whole continent, all the bubble and boil and onrush of frontier settlement, sent the tide brimming across the Sabine into Haden's colony.

The district now had several thousand settlers. There were Spaniards, Mexicans, Frenchmen, Americans, Indians, free Negroes, and slaves—from sober industrious folk to the most lawless men of the Western world.

Austin's colonists, all screened for ability and character, had settled virgin country where there had been no Mexican farmers. Only one serious conflict with a native landowner had ever arisen.

But Edwards bit his teeth into a half-lawless, nonrooted society, a hodgepodge of many nationalities, rich and poor, free and slave, good and evil. Such a society would snarl back. Even with a man more wise, just, and tactful than rawboned Edwards at the helm, trouble would be inevitable. He was a hotheaded, heedless man, whose knobby joints swelled easily with anger.

He had ordered all established settlers to present their titles, threatening to dispossess them, an authority he did not have. Few titles were perfect, and a storm arose. He discriminated against Mexicans and the poor in favor of Americans. Citizens and veterans of the Mexican revolution angrily demanded of the legislature why they should be ruled by "a foreign *empresario*." They threatened to toss Edwards back into the United States.

Edwards, a perfect china-shop bull and bully, came out "in a herricane," as he expressed it, and "sounded the trump." He bellowed that he would send troublemakers "in irons" to far-off Saltillo. When the authorities refused to back up his illegal arrogance, his masked raiders arrested the mayor and the militia head and gave them a kangaroo trial.

Presently Haden's brother led a group of armed Americans and Indians under a red-and-white flag inscribed "Independence, Liberty and Justice" to seize the Nacogdoches Stone House on the plaza and proclaimed "the Republic of Fredonia."

Austin's orderly colony was endangered. The disorder ran counter to everything for which he had labored. He had tried to inscribe his slogan "Fidelity to Mexico" in the hearts and homes of his people. The phrase was constantly on his lips and was carried on the masthead of the San Felipe newspaper. He had built his colony on the solid rock of progress and mutual understanding with Mexicans. He had worked discreetly within the law. When necessary he had carried his grievances quietly to legislature, Congress, governors, military commanders, cabinet ministers, even to the president. By persistent tact he had won over an official foe, Governor Trespalacios.

Now the wild men and land-grabbers near the Louisiana frontier were storming in and out of Nacogdoches, guns in hand, threatening peace and security. Such rebel violence was bound to draw more and more troops into Texas, which might provoke new conflicts.

Mexican fears were great, for the rebellion coincided with demands in United States newspapers that Texas be taken by purchase or force. The American representative in Mexico City, Joel R. Poinsett, was backing dubious land claims and still scheming to alienate Texas, and the United States government was pressuring Mexico to sell Texas. Large companies had bought up Texas land grants, in spite of specific clauses that they were not transferable to foreigners or foreign companies, and were selling vast quantities of worthless stock and scrip for acreage they had no right to sell, often for many more millions of acres than the area claimed. Plain swindles!

The Mexican authorities feared that the fleeced buyers would blame Mexico, not the grafters, and that the United States government would be forced to pull wormy chestnuts out of the fire. Mexican fears of foreign intrigue rose to hatred and threatened all American colonization. Mexican fears were now given body by the crazy Fredonian revolt. The trouble threatened the whole edifice that Austin had erected.

Repeatedly Steve warned Haden that his insults to Mexico and his "wild talk and boasting" of what he would do to settlers lacking clear titles would blow back in his face. "Your present imprudent course . . . will injure all the new settlements." Harshly he added, "The people in your quarter" seem to have "run mad or worse . . . destroying themselves, building up the creed of their enemies . . . jeopardizing the prospects of hundreds of innocent families who wish to live in peace."

Conflict was now inevitable. Saucedo rushed troops from San Antonio. He and Steve were now face to face in San Felipe.

2

Steve gave the political chief the latest news. The new Fredonian republic had made a treaty with a minor Cherokee chief which gave the Indians all Texas to the west.

"The Fredonians have gone mad," said Stephen hotly, "to endanger the lives of the women and children of our colony. Fortunately, the most influential Cherokee chiefs refused to recognize the pact and ordered those who did, to be seized and punished.

"I told the Fredonians," Stephen went on, "they had made a terrible blunder and that they would get no help from the United States. I warned them that the people of my colony unanimously disapproved and were faithful as one man to the government of their adopted country."

"We admit we were worried," Saucedo remarked.

"I warned Haden that any Fredonian agent would be thrown out of this colony bodily and that, as a Mexican citizen and an officer, I would sacrifice my life before I would violate my duty and my oath of office."

"But will your people back you?" asked Ahumada, who returned just then, spurs clanking. He slapped his broad-brimmed military hat against his leg to shake the rain off.

"I have ordered them to help expel the uprisers from Mexican soil. Pending your orders, I have called for thirty volunteers to go with your men to take Nacogdoches. All will fight and fight hard. 'You are now Mexicans,' I told them, 'and you owe the same duties to the country of your adoption that you once owed to that of your nativity.'"

The two officials were touched by Stephen's warm sentiments in favor of Mexico. Other townsfolk had drifted in to listen, and the group now toasted Mexico, the president, the constitution, and each other.

The weather continued bad; dismal rain made it impossible to get heavy supplies across the swollen streams. But in spite of the downpour, Stephen's volunteers and others from settlements on Galveston Bay kept drifting in, not merely 30 men but 100 and, to Steve's vast surprise, finally more than 400; all were aching for a good fight. A 4-pounder, left at the mouth of the Colorado by an early vessel, had been dragged along to be used to knock down the Stone House.

The Americans encamped alongside the 800 Mexican soldiers on the bluff.

There were considerable hard drinking, gambling, and boasting but only a few fights. The Americans swapped knives and whistles and mirrors for horsehair belts and bright kerchiefs and sashes. Even watches, saddles, and blankets were traded. They tried Mexican food, *tortillas* smeared with red-hot chili: some swallowed it with gusto; others spat it out amid yells and laughter. At night the two forces gathered separately or together around the camp-fires.

Cowboy and vaquero and border melodies floated across through the endless rain.

The delay and bad weather got on everybody's nerves. Austin and Coles, the alcalde, were kept busy rounding up food and supplies, a heavy drain on the colonists' resources. Saucedo and Ahumada vowed angrily that they would string up the whole crew of revolters to the last man. Steve urged that as little blood as possible be spilled. Calm justice would win the loyal support of all the border people to the government.

Under his urging, Ahumada sent word to the rebellious Cherokee that they could obtain government land whenever they indicated what they wanted. It took more effort to get him to offer a full pardon to Haden Edwards and all others willing to lay down their arms immediately.

But Edwards shouted back that the Fredonians would never yield one inch till they had won independence from the Sabine to the Rio Grande.

The skies cleared, the ground grew solid, and the rivers dropped. The prospect of action restored good spirits. Red kerchiefs were knotted about brown throats. Jingling bridles were pushed over horses' ears; squeaking saddles were cinched tight. Soon the troops, shouting, singing, and waving their big hats, swam the river with their horses. The little ferry shuttled back and forth all day with supplies.

They moved northeast along the San Antonio Trace, the old Camino Real, that Steve and Seguín had followed, through the forests, across the prairies, and over the flooded rivers.

At night, when the three leaders sat around the fire before their tents, Austin told of things being done in his colony; grants were being given for cotton gins, sawmills, and other enterprises. New Orleans brokers considered Texas cotton better than sea-island cotton.

They discussed slavery and religious tolerance and trade. Steve brought up the matter which most irked the settlers. Mexican law provided no trial by jury. All but minor criminal and civil cases had to be reviewed in far-off Saltillo. This meant weeks of travel and a delay of months, even years, and was a hardship to both the community and the accused, especially poorer people.

It took the troops all day to cross the broad Trinity River. They moved on more cautiously. Ahumada sent out an advance patrol to join a volunteer force from Galveston Bay.

The patrol galloped right into Nacogdoches itself. The plaza was deserted, silent as a tomb. The Stone House was empty.

Panicky at the approach of federal troops and Austin's colonists, bringing bullets not aid, the fire-eating rebels had melted away. The rebel Cherokee chief and a shady American trader were captured and killed by the Cherokee themselves. The whole affair, so serious a few weeks earlier, became comic opera.

Dashing on to the Sabine, the advance patrol captured nine men with only a single shot. Following Steve's advice, Ahumada merely questioned the prisoners and released them without punishment. He confiscated only the property of several leaders. Steve wrote a friend that the colonel's moderation had put Mexico high in the good opinion of the world. "My own admiration is boundless."

He sent his militia home immediately and was anxious to hurry back himself, but Ahumada insisted that he stay on as interpreter and adviser. They went clear to the Sabine into every settlement.

The American colonizers, even squatters without titles, struck Ahumada favorably. He exclaimed repeatedly over the progress in roads, fences, cleared fields, houses, crops, herds, mills. Such hard-working people should be given titles promptly or be well compensated for all improvements. In consultation with Steve he penned an able constructive report.

Austin had done his duty as a Mexican citizen, as an officer, and as a man of business enterprise. He had also proved that his people were loyally behind him and the government of their adopted country. But Mexico was now frightened and suspicious of all Americans. If revolt had happened once, it might again. A strong garrison was set up in Nacogdoches, and more and more troops came into East Texas. From this time on, ever-stronger measures, not always wise or just, tried to halt American immigration, to set up tight frontier control, and to bind Texas closer to Mexico.

Steve met growing hostility on all sides just because he was a foreigner. Collisions between Mexicans and Americans, between two rival peoples and governments, multiplied. This was to make Austin's long task of conciliation ever more difficult and, in the end, impossible.

10 · Death and Loneliness

VOICES MADE A GREAT HUBBUB in Buck Pettus's steaming bar. A lanky hog raiser slammed down his glass and shouted, "I'll never pay one cent of them new taxes. We'll have a Boston Tea Party scrap of it. We'll come armed and show Steve Austin whether he will collect. We will tar and feather him."

A chorus of approval echoed his words.

Steve had hoped that the first elections in the colony, held in February, 1828, would lighten his load and give him time to wind up his three new grants to settle 900 more families. But if anything, self-government seemed to create even more problems for him and to bring old grievances out into the open.

A state constitution had finally been adopted, and the settlers had been asked to choose their own officials: an alcalde, an *ayuntamiento* of governing *regidores*, and local *comisarios* and *síndicos*. The *comisario*, a sort of combined sheriff, clerk, and justice of the peace, had to keep the census and records of travelers, help tax collectors, carry out the orders of the *regidores* and the alcalde, and arrest lawbreakers. The *síndico* was a combined notary and prosecuting attorney.

For the *ayuntamiento* Steve had proposed men near San Felipe who could meet regularly. But those elected came from such remote places that they got together for but one meeting.

The new city hall, where they held that first session, was an unfinished log house behind the Whiteside Hotel that had no roof against rain and no windows against the wind. Its walls were not even chinked up.

At that one bitter cold reunion, they listened to Steve's report and approved the district charter he had drawn up but did little else except petition the legislature to allow slaves to be brought in as "contract" laborers.

The new charter provided for local taxes to maintain the government. Complainers at once gathered in the grogshop, angrily criticizing Steve's land fees, the boundaries of their properties, the continuation of heavy fines for drunkenness and profanity, and the new taxes.

Free frontier folk were always irked by the wisest regulations, but now they "growled and grumbled and muttered without knowledge why or without being able to explain why." Steve often chided them for their "childish pettiness," their "rage at trifles."

"I do not complain too much," he told Bell. "It is human nature."

If good men were inborn grumblers and rebels, bad men were often malicious. Many crooks, soreheads, and incompetents had slipped through the bars into the colony.

"The grumblers," Austin noted, "are those who have more to say and less to lose either of property or character." And he remarked to a friend, "I was foolish indeed to allow my fancy to wander in the Elysian fields of imagined success." There were still problems to be solved.

He called a public meeting and patiently explained the purpose of the new taxes and why he should not be required to pay all administration costs any longer. The Spanish secretary was paid $1,000; a few hundred dollars were needed for records, stationery, fuel, and rent; and $400 were to be set aside for Indian and post-office matters. If births went unrecorded, settlers' children would lose important privileges as native-born Mexicans. A town hall and a jail had to be built.

He ended by telling them sharply that the law had to be obeyed. "One of these days you will have officials less likely to be as patient as a dray horse and less willing to stand for as much abuse as I have for the sake of the common good."

Boundaries and titles still caused disputes. Bell himself journeyed up from Columbia to San Felipe to complain that he had expected that his plot of land would reach to the San Bernardo River, but the final survey left a sliver of land between.

"It's no good to anybody else," he said.

"You can have it," said Steve wearily. "I'll fix it up somehow."

2

Wild accusations over Steve's land fees continued. As a result the Mexican authorities cut the fees in half, with great loss to him.

"Who is going to pay me for administering the grant all these years? For feeding the Indians to keep them friendly?" Steve asked Bell.

"I have paid for poor folk out of my own pocket. I have enriched many a man who has never paid me one red cent, who got his land absolutely free, for whom I paid the surveying and the filing charges and the cost of the deed. Yet these same ones now accuse me of cheating, speculation, and self-enrichment. It is incredible!

"All I have, Josiah, is part of my premium lands, perhaps not even half. I have not even been able to pay all my own debts, those of my father and Bryan, or the losses on those confounded lead mines and the Arkansas land deals."

One large sum was owed to grasping Anthony Butler for slaves hired long ago in the lead mines. Butler, engaged in Texas land speculation, was soon to become United States minister to Mexico. Steve still had to repay Lovelace the $500. General Wavell had advanced money to Steve during difficult days in Mexico. He had been seized by pirates and Steve wished to reimburse him. The Joe Hawkins claim still had to be settled.

The Hawkins lawyer, General John Mason, showed up with fiery young Edmund St. John Hawkins, not yet of age, to claim that Joe had put $30,000 into the venture.

"You know that is absurd," Steve told young Edmund.

"I'm eternally grateful to your father and his early help. I owe him far more than the small sums he advanced, more than what you claim. But I can't pay it. He had to take potluck with me, and after all the misery I went through, he is scarcely entitled to more than I have made. I have only losses to show. In spite of my losses that land will always be his. Someday it will be worth a lot more than what you are claiming."

But Edmund, as Steve recalled, had always been headstrong and full of sullen resentments. Now he was in the clutches of General Mason, a greedy, unscrupulous man with little of the milk of human kindness.

Steve went to great pains to draw up a precise bill of particulars before he argued it out with Mason. The lawyer claimed that Steve was liable for Hawkins's losses in private trading in Mexico and for the usurers' interest for money he had borrowed when he had gone bankrupt. These two items made up the bulk of the claim.

"I am not liable for one penny of either," said Steve. "Joe promised to put in $4,000. He was to get half the premium lands and half of all profit. But he never completed his agreement. He never paid in more than $1,600. Besides there have been no colony profits, only losses and big ones."

Mason argued that this did not relieve Steve from liability for Hawkins's own losses. He had incurred heavy interest obligations because of the money raised for Steve. He insisted that the goods sent to Mexico were part of the colony enterprise, a contribution to the joint effort.

"If he engaged in trading on his own initiative and for personal profit, that is no concern of mine or of the colony, none whatever," retorted Steve. "But if you insist, then I will make Hawkins's estate liable for every penny of loss. I have made up those losses with money from later colonies in which Hawkins held no interest. Joe did no work. If you press me, I shall have to demand full personal compensation for the exploring and settling by Moses and myself, for the full expense of that year in Mexico, and for the cost of administering the colony. I will take a salary besides. I will hold you liable for the paying of the militia and for my entertaining of the Indians and all my gifts to them. Besides that, my slave Richmond, worth at least $800, was sold as part of the Hawkins estate. I'll put in a bill for his hire and value. I lost two-thirds of the value of the *Lively*. The estate will owe a vast sum."

They argued back and forth. "I still hold Joe's premium lands, over 30,000 acres. They are still in my name. I have considered them inviolate and sacred, part of my debt of gratitude to Joe Hawkins. I no longer have any obligation to deed them over to him or to his heirs. But I will gladly do so whenever an authorized member of the family, not a minor like Edmund here, but an adult, can validate the claim legally by living on them the minimum time required to establish title."

"You mean you won't deed them over if I live on the land," demanded Edmund angrily.

"You aren't of age, Edmund."

When neither Mason nor Edmund would give ground, Steve lost patience. "Very well. Take the matter to court. It will be settled in Saltillo by the Supreme Court. That will take years and will cost you plenty. In the end I will get judgment for all the losses of the colony, all my personal losses, and for unpaid salary against the estate and any property of the survivors. That will come to far more than the value of the land I offer as almost a free gift. It will mean that nobody will get anything. You will not only get no land, but, Edmund, you will be loaded down with such heavy obligations that you will never get ahead in Texas."

For the first time Edmund vacillated, and Steve said more gently, "Go down there on the property, Edmund. I'll survey your share for you, and I'll make out a deed when you are twenty-one, and we'll make it stick. I'll help you get ahead in every way I can."

In the end Edmund accepted this proposal. The land was near the new bustling port of Brazoria on the lower Brazos, and Edmund did well. A few years later he became a town official.

3

Steve was very happy when his cousin Mary Holley wrote that she intended to visit Texas. He corresponded with her steadily and owed many of his liberal ideas to her. She was a cultured woman, the widow of the president of the University of Transylvania, which Steve had attended, and had written articles and books and had composed and published music. She was now a governess in New Orleans. But he had to warn her that she would find Texas pretty rough.

"I am still living in a log cabin with no comforts, and I am soured with the world." He was forever doomed to serve the settlers, who did not even thank him for his "care and labor," let alone pay what they owed him, although his own creditors pressed remorselessly. But a "puncheon hut" or an "Indian camp" was but a trifle if a steppingstone to "a comfortable home and a farm for life."

He was still midway on a long flight of steppingstones. With all his duties and worries and, presently, new serious difficulties with the government, Steve's brow grew furrowed and his countenance dreary.

James's new wife, Eliza, wrote to Emily in Missouri that Stephen's excessive devotion to his colony had pulled him down to "a mere shadow." If he does not "ride about and take more exercise, his life will be short." James also wrote Emily that Steve, though only thirty-five, "begins to look quite old, and the wrinkles are becoming plainer daily."

Ever since Fredonia his spirit had been dark. Nothing had gone smoothly since that fracas. Ever since then the authorities had been suspicious, and new regulations constantly harassed the settlers. His return to the colony that year of the Fredonian trouble had been sad. Baron de Bastrop, he learned, was dead.

Bastrop had helped Steve every step, and for months they had worked side by side on the Colorado in harmony and affection. Steve's greatest mainstay in Mexico was gone, and he was cast into deep gloom.

Often Steve felt ill. Dr. Sibley prescribed medicines by long distance, but in the summer of 1829 Steve came down with fever and for weeks hovered between life and death.

When he could sit up for brief spells, his spirits still remained low. His deep personal losses—the death of his father, mother, and other relatives, the loss of his best friends, Joe Hawkins and Bastrop—darkened his spirit.

Now came a worse blow. James died suddenly in New Orleans.

His brother, able to mix with Mexicans in easier friendliness than Steve could, had proved most useful to Bastrop in lobbying at the Saltillo capital to quash legislation injurious to the colony. Many duties had been lifted from Steve's shoulders by James's energy and gay humor. He had gotten a Brazos farm going excellently and had married and sired a child, whom he named Stephen. Numerous trading enterprises had turned out profitably.

Early one morning in late summer, 1829, James bumped into a sea-captain friend on Charles Street in New Orleans. They shared glasses at Swanson's Café and agreed to meet again that evening. James complained of a bad headache, and his friend chided him for running about in the New Orleans sun without an umbrella.

James laughed. "Anybody who can stand Texas sun can stand Hades."

But about one o'clock he was seized with stomach pains and by three in the morning was dead.

The melancholy news delayed Steve's full recovery.

His hopes and prospects had been blasted, he wrote. "I have passed a truly slavish life here for nine years, my constitution is broken, my health is bad, and my days are probably drawing to a close."

A whole year after James's death, widow Eliza wrote Emily that Steve had "a gloomy melancholy look. If you were here to tease and plague him, he might show a more smiling countenance."

11 · Closing the Doors

STEVE'S THOUGHTS TURNED to Emily. "I am quite alone here. My beloved brother is no more," he wrote her husband James Perry. He urged him to come with Emily and the children and set up his merchandising business in Texas. After November 1, 1830, no more goods could be brought in duty-free.

I have picked an eleven league tract of land for you on Galveston Bay—over 50,000 acres. The deep forests, streams and harbors will be good for a steam sawmill. Lumber can't be imported and it is selling in Vera Cruz for the phenomenal price of fifty to eighty dollars a thousand.

To gain title, besides coming in person within two years, about a $1000 will be required for fees and filing. I can advance this to you as a four-to-six year loan.

He did not mention that he himself was shouldering all surveying costs.

The tract will provide for all my nieces and nephews—half for you, Perry, and half for Emily's children by Bryan. I wish all my sister's children provided for. The large ranch in James' name will be a handsome provision for his baby, little Stephen.

Shortly before his illness, he had again toyed with the idea of marriage and wrote a second time about Miss Williams in Columbia. His Tennessee friend replied that Steve would have "little trouble" with the widow. There were also many other "maids and widows . . . who would make your heart go pitapat" and would emigrate to any part of the world with a clever fellow. If Stephen could be satisfied with "beauty, good temper and affectionate disposition," his friend promised to fix it so he could "lay siege forthwith."

But his illness and piled-up duties drove the wife idea out of his head. He wrote Perry that he was never likely to marry.

All my property will go to your children. I never urged you to come before this because till now I was never so thoroughly convinced of the future rapid rise of this country. You have no idea of it or you would be here before April, family and all. Bring all manner and great quantity of fruit seeds . . . gooseberry and raspberry roots, in particular. Furniture is scarce and high. Bring in enough to be comfortable.

A few head of English cattle should be brought. "Nature never made a better place for a stock farm than this land I have asked for you." He followed this up with letter after letter.

Receiving no assurances that Perry would come, Steve's spirits remained low. On March 12, 1830, he urged settlers to hurry to take out their titles quickly as his health was not good and he might die. Fortunately he had found an invaluable assistant, Sam Williams, who became a member of the *ayuntamiento* and took detailed work off his shoulders.

Though half doubting that his brother-in-law would come, Steve went down to Davis Point on the land that he had selected for Perry with a surveyor. A stranger on a mule rode toward him around the head of the bayou. He was a short, prosy individual with narrow eyes and uneasy glance. Steve put him down instantly as a tenderfoot.

"Stephen Austin?" he asked stiffly, touching his hat. "I am your brother-in-law, James Perry."

"Marvelous!" cried Steve, watching Perry get off his mule with a grimace from sore muscles. "I'm just measuring off your land for you."

Perry drew a deep breath as he looked at the Gulf and the circle of woods. "It's really beautiful, isn't it? How did you decide what I might like?" he added with a belligerency that Steve did not notice.

Steve stayed on for ten days surveying the tract. Perry went up to San Felipe. He thought it a pleasant place. The woods were beautiful. There were some thirty houses now and another small tavern. The weekly *Texas Gazette*, started by Godwin Brown Cotton, was now a year old; the subscription fee could be paid in cash or produce. Noah Smithwick, the local cutler and gunsmith, who had started from Kentucky in 1827 with one change of clothing and a rifle, was now gaining fame as one of the talents of the frontier.

Steve wrote Emily in high spirits about "the singular

coincidence" that Perry had found him "on the very spot" where they would likely spend a large part of the rest of their lives.

He is delighted with the situation, and I think you also will be. I am really happy at the idea of your leaving that cold region. I'll give the girls something pretty and the boys ponies and a little boat. They will have their full of fishing and hunting. Fowls are numerous, and oysters are at the door.

Bring all books belonging to Moses and Bryan. We must provide a teacher to educate the children well. All should learn Spanish. By the time they come on to the stage, Texas will present a fine field for men of education and talents.

He joined Perry in San Felipe. Disquieting news had come through from Mexico City. Brutal military coups had occurred. General Anastacio Bustamante had smashed into control, and President Vicente Guerrero was treacherously murdered. But Steve had always gotten on well with Don Anastacio and hoped for the best.

On April 6, 1830, like a bolt from the blue, came a law that was to shake Austin's colony, destroy other uncompleted colonies, and change the destiny of Texas. The law contained liberal trade features, but it suspended all land grants unless 100 colonists had already been settled. Only the first Austin grant and the Green DeWitt colony just west had brought in that many families. Would the new policy stop Steve's new grants from being settled?

"What will the law do to my grant?" Perry asked.

"It is not a colony, and we can prove you were on it before the law was passed. But things are tightening up. You had better settle as soon as possible."

2

The unfavorable law had been passed at the behest of
the new military commandant of the Northwest, General
Manuel de Mier y Terán. Alarmed at the danger of losing
Texas, he had proposed stern military occupation, settlement by Europeans, and closer trade ties for Texas with
the rest of Mexico.

Worried as to how the San Felipe colonists, many of
whom had relatives expecting to settle in Texas, would re-
act to the new law, both President Bustamante and Mier
y Terán wrote Steve cordially.

To the president, Austin replied tartly. Was it the aim of
"such a cruel . . . unjust" law to destroy the happiness of
the colony for which the president had always shown such
"friendship and protection"? He hoped to receive a reas-
suring reply by return mail.

He wrote Mier y Terán that he expected settlers for his
new grants would not be turned back. "My immigrants to
Texas never cost the government one penny—only permission to settle the wilderness. They have never been
aided or protected by the government." He sent similar
letters to other Mexican officials.

By early June many of Steve's immigrants had reached
the frontier. He wrote directly to Colonel José de las
Piedras at Nacogdoches, in charge of customs and immigration, asking him to allow them to proceed. "All is peace
in this settlement," Steve wrote pointedly. "Local authorities should help keep all Texas in peace."

Piedras agreed with Steve's interpretation, and Mier y

Terán ordered that all Austin certificates of settlement be honored as passports.

But other *empresarios* and settlers, who had set out before learning about the new law, suffered hardships, arrest, and deportation. The law left big speculating land companies in the United States without a leg for their manipulations, a loss of millions for them and unsuspecting suckers. Angered that Steve's new colonies had been exempted, other promoters accused him of getting the law passed in order to crush all rivals. The more fraudulent the land company claims, the harsher were their accusations of Steve.

"They will find themselves gnawing on a file," he remarked. "I have been the only *empresario* performing his duty and obeying the law."

Loud threats by newer, jingoistic settlers mingled with louder cries for the seizure of Texas. Anti-Mexican propaganda broke out in a red rash in the American press. All the pro-Jackson papers and others were constantly shouting, "We must have Texas—by force or purchase." Official Washington pressure on Mexico to sell Texas increased considerably.

Mexicans saw the North as a giant "silently" expanding at their expense. Mier y Terán sent word to Congress that the colonists were flouting the religious laws. Actually Steve had run out several Methodist preachers who had celebrated illegal services, and heated, anti-Mexican, Protestant propaganda was added to that of the land speculators.

In good part Steve blamed the arbitrary law on Poinsett's unpopular meddling in Mexican affairs. "What evils have resulted from the intrigues attributed to

Poinsett!" he wrote Colonel Piedras. Poinsett, the American representative in Mexico City, also had private land schemes, which led the Mexican government to suspect that the United States government was secretly a colonizer. "The idea of seeing such a country as this overrun by a slave population almost makes me weep." But to say anything to his own settlers about slavery's injustice or its "demoralizing effects on society" was "to draw down ridicule." Without slavery this "fair region" could be made "the Eden of America." Texas should remain Mexican, for thereby it would enjoy greater growth and freedom. Union with the United States would make it a slave state.

Steve urged friends in the North to present the Mexican side boldly in the newspapers and suggested that they get the famed frontier chronicler, Timothy Flint, to do an honest book on Texas.

3

The arbitrary new restrictions did not accomplish the ends sought by Mexico. Reliable settlers were excluded, but shiftless adventurers, crooks, criminals, and all the plotters wanting to annex the territory to the United States slipped through in droves. Secret agents like Sam Houston and adventurers like James Bowie, a former filibuster, came in. Also thousands of primitive bellicose Indians were being shoved out of the United States into Texas. The number of savages was growing faster than the civilizers.

At the first breathing spell, Steve engaged a man to put up a small brick house so that the Perrys would get through the first winter comfortably.

"There are now a hundred troops on the Brazos at the upper San Antonio road," he wrote Emily. "That would be a good point for Perry to set up a store."

Steve sent Perry a long list of things he wanted. The law required him to have a uniform, infantry color; gold epaulets; a gold- or yellow-mounted sword; also a sword sash and belt, yellow-mounted. "I also want a navy blue military surtout with standing collar handsomely though plainly trimmed with black cord, and pantaloons trimmed in the same manner," a "scarlet waistcoat" edged with gold cord, and a pair of boots and yellow spurs. He also asked for a handsome set of holsters, and a "yellow-bitted bridle."

"During the ten years I have spent in Texas, . . . few books have come within my reach." He was "greatly in need" of Waite's *State Papers* and Vattel's *Law of Nations* in Spanish and also the constitutions and legal codes of Colombia, Buenos Aires, Chile, Peru, and Bolivia. He ordered subscriptions to the *National Gazette* and the *Quarterly Review*. Steve had given a completed map of Texas to a Philadelphia publisher to be published cost free. In return the publisher should be willing to give Perry one of the best bound American atlases. It would be "useful to teach the children geography." He needed a portable writing desk, a large, plain secretary, and a bookcase in which to keep his private papers. He hoped they would arrive before Christmas.

A letter from Perry jolted him back on his heels. A new "fine son" born to Emily in his absence made it impossible for them to move out this fall; the south country was too subject to fever and cholera. Wryly, he added that he did not want to go to Texas on any "wild goose chase." Perry was not satisfied with Steve's arbitrary selection of a site and felt that, in deeding half the land to Emily for Bryan's children, Steve had intended a slight on his treatment of his stepchildren. "With regard to those children," he wrote hotly, "I have always done for them and by them as well as I would have or could have done if they had been my own."

Few men have ever had a chance to get 50,000 acres scot free on a great river and harbor in a new growing country, but Perry wrote only nagging complaints, no thanks at all.

Grievously disappointed, Steve replied that, if Perry did not like the land selected, the cream of the coast, he was welcome to any acres he himself owned, even his prize Peach Point tract where he expected someday to retire.

Far from having implied neglect for Bryan's children, he was grateful for Perry's fine care and merely wished to do something for them also. Only by taking the land in the name of two families had he been able to obtain such a large grant.

I'm laboring more for yours and Emily's children than for myself—what do I want with property or fortune? . . . Little will do me, and every year less for I am daily getting more tired of the world and its intercourse and affairs. . . .

This will be my last try at helping any relative. But if you were here this winter you could collect two hundred cows and calves owed me, sufficient to start a good farm. I need you to take care of my pecuniary affairs or I will be as poor as a church mouse. But do as you please, only let me know if you are not coming so I can make other plans.

4

Christmas Day found Steve, not enjoying dinner with the Perrys, but on the long road to San Antonio with a Mexican servant.

He had been elected to represent Texas in the legislature at Saltillo. He had not wished for this, but his nomination had been pushed by the Mexicans of La Bahía and San Antonio for whom he had often acted as land agent without cost.

He dreaded placing himself within reach of the politicians. At Saltillo he would have a bed of thorns. Though prejudices against the United States were subsiding, "uninformed persons still believed Poinsett was the United States government" and that all North Americans were "connected with his intrigues. This may make my new post at Saltillo unpleasant, even critical. But I hope an honest . . . prudent course will carry me safely through the many difficulties."

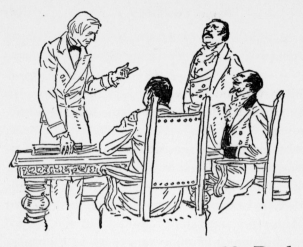

12 · Dark Clouds

In San Antonio, Steve saw friends briefly. The new political chief, Ramón Músquiz, was an old friend from New Orleans days. Seguín was now ranching 30 miles out, but he hurried into the city.

Veramendi, now Vice-Governor of Coahuila-Texas, was in Saltillo. The Veramendis' farm was in a flutter, for their lovely daughter Ursula, now twenty, was about to marry dashing James Bowie.

This young redheaded giant who went everywhere with a coal-black slave as gigantic as himself was an adventurous, carousing bravo not much to Steve's taste. Earlier in the year, passing through San Felipe, he had presented to Steve a letter of introduction. He was wearing his famous bowie knife—a new one made by Noah Smithwick, of San Felipe.

It was a weapon contrived years before by one of his brothers, and with it Jim Bowie had carved his way to fame as the most daring man of the lower Mississippi. He was ever ready to fight shady gamblers, rescue damsels in distress, or punish any imagined slight. His favorite mode of dueling was to slash with a knife held in his right hand while his left wrist was tied to that of his opponent. He had disemboweled or punctured many a man, and his own huge frame was laced with scars from bullets and knives.

With two brothers he had operated a big Louisiana plantation and a sawmill. Then he took up slave running. At Jean Laffite's Galveston hide-out, he bought Africans at a dollar a pound, roped them together, and lashed them into Louisiana. This risky smuggling required courage, greed, and at times murderous brutality. Later he had joined a filibuster foray into Mexico.

He had just come back from Saltillo, where with his father-in-law-to-be he had been building a cotton mill. He had persuaded officials to make him a Mexican citizen so that he could qualify under the new land law, and he had tucked fifteen 11-league grants—750,000 acres—into his vest pocket. Steve feared that this type of speculation rather than sound settlement would mean trouble for everybody.

Steve left San Antonio with a military escort across desolate mesquite and sagebrush country, full of rattlers, coyotes, prairie dogs, and goatherds, into dangerous Lipan and Apache country.

He reached the old city of Saltillo on January 13 and found quarters with Father Músquiz, a cousin of the political chief. Steve's fellow deputies at the stately Palacio del Gobierno, across from the cathedral on small Independence Plaza, seemed unusually friendly.

At Governor José María Viesca's house he met Father

Miguel Muldoon, the new General Vicarate of Texas, who was planning to locate in San Felipe. He was a close friend of Minister Alamán and General Mier y Terán. Steve wrote Sam Williams that, if the government had wished to harass them, it would not have chosen a man "so liberal and enlightened on religious subjects." Though accustomed to the best society of Mexico and the nobility and gentry of Europe, Muldoon seemed eager to adapt himself to the back country and take his fees in produce. He had obtained a large piece of land, about 70,000 acres, and looked to Texas as "his only home." Sam should entertain him, help him select good acreage, and build a vicarage.

Every few weeks Steve saw more Mexican troops streaming north toward Texas. Before he had left the colony, strong garrisons had been placed in and around the farms and on the coast. It was also rumored that Mexico was shipping criminals north to Texas as settlers.

In a letter to the new Coahuila-Texas representative in Congress in Mexico City, Steve asked bluntly whether Indian danger in Texas could be scotched by garrisons or by the increase in the number of civilized people. The 1830 law caused the savage and criminal population to grow faster. In spite of the large number of federal troops, several settlers recently had been murdered by Indians.

If the government would authorize a mounted cavalry company, Steve promised to organize it within a month —officers, horses, and arms—and it would quickly stop depredations. He urged repeal of the immigration restrictions. Let goods enter Texas duty-free for five years more. Pay the soldiers promptly. Organize the mobile cavalry unit.

In the *Texas Gazette*, Steve sought to quiet the fears of the settlers. The 1830 law did not affect the present colony and would aid all Texas trade and industry. The heavy troop movements were not against the colonists but for the protection of the frontier. They would bring freedom from Indian attacks and unpleasant militia duty and provide markets for products.

Much of the new friction was due to the Galveston Bay and Land Company, which had illegally gobbled up half a dozen private grants, including those of Steve's Mexico City friend, Zavala. This outfit had pushed fraudulent speculation, selling unlimited stock and scrip in disregard of Mexican law. The 1830 law had put them on the hot seat, and they were moving heaven and earth to get individual and total land claims validated. William S. Parott, one of Steve's companions on his first exploration trips, was in Mexico City trying to get one of the company's smaller grants reinstated. Colonel José Antonio Mexía appealed to Austin to help him. Steve answered cordially but said frankly he would aid only legitimate settlement. In defiance of the law Zavala was bringing in two boatloads of foreign immigrants with seeds and tools. The government warned that they would be "repelled by force."

Again Austin was blamed. He credited the false report on "snakes in the grass around San Felipe."

2

A ticklish dispute arose over land titles on the Trinity River where remnants of Laffite's pirate band and filibus-

ter forays had settled. They had been promised titles, but
General Mier y Terán placed large military contingents
at Velasco at the mouth of the Brazos and at Anahuac a
mile up the Trinity, the latter under Colonel John Davis
Bradburn, a vain, hotheaded, highhanded officer who soon
clashed with both the civil authorities and the squatters
and made many arbitrary arrests.

Steve sympathized with the settlers but wrote Sam not
to let his own colonists get embroiled in outside quarrels.

We have to play the turtle, head within our own shell . . . no
opinion—no advice. . . . General Mier is our mainstay . . .
worthy of our confidence and support. Keep dead silence. If
the settlers refuse to heed firebrands, the dark clouds over the
Trinity will pass away.

New legislation now closed nearly all Texas ports to
foreigners. Steve wrote Williams to publish the "absurd"
law but to make no comment beyond inquiring whether it
violated the constitution. "Constantly stress the sacredness
of that instrument," he advised.

Matamoros, the leading northwestern port was soon
paralyzed and in an uproar. They really are "closing the
ports," Steve wrote.

Poca importa—they cannot build a wall across them all. As
I told the good folks here, which they took very ill . . . the law
of nature has a just right to break down all walls that are . . .
notorious public nuisances.

But Governor Viesca was hostile. "He hates foreigners
as he hates the devil. . . . He is refusing to confirm the
titles of anybody but native-born Mexicans." Steve urged
Sam Williams to hurry up and finish his second colony of

500 settlers. Fortunately the land commissioner there had full power to issue final titles. To avoid trouble, Sam and he should go ahead without consulting anybody.

There was a prospect of another revolution. "God help preserve this unhappy . . . distracted nation," Steve wrote. Once more he urged caution. The settlers should keep out of the new "scramble," or they would get trampled on "like children in a mob" by friends and foes alike. Neutrality would injure neither band, and maybe they would be left alone.

3

Steve was not comfortable in Saltillo. The weather was dreary, heavy rains and three snows of from 4 to 6 inches. The damp, moldy adobe and stone houses struck chill to the marrow. There was no heat in homes or in the thick-walled Chamber of Deputies, a perfect icebox, where the legislators sat bundled in capes and blankets, coughing and sneezing. Steve came down with several bad colds. His health was poor.

But worse than discomfort was the antiforeign hatred. He was determined to get a proper court system for Texas and at the start had reported enthusiastically that his harmonious understanding with his colleagues was going to bring success. But he soon discovered that cordiality was a mask that barely concealed a hatred of foreigners so deep that his very presence was resented.

Coahuila, more populous than Texas, had the overwhelming majority, but it was jealous of the rich fast-growing northern area of the state and opposed everything put forward by Texas. "Nothing need be expected from the Legislature," Steve wrote. "All I calculate on is to pass away the time . . . silently and get back as soon as I can."

Texas, he now realized, had to have statehood, or it would be strangled by the militaristic federal government.

Bitterly he wrote Minister Alamán and General Mier y Terán that Texas, chained to Coahuila, could expect no justice, no courts, no trial by jury. For the time being, slaves should be allowed in from countries already having slavery. "Don't cut off immigration. Above all, don't close the ports. That will be our ruin." If permitted, Texas could export thousands of bales of cotton the coming season.

Alamán wrote back that any plan to make Texas a separate Mexican state would go down better with Congress if it were worked out amicably with Coahuila.

Mier y Terán, though opposed to the slightest further concession to slavery, answered that Steve should not be downcast. "Reforms are never won in a day."

Holy Week brought legislative idleness in Saltillo. All stores were closed tight, and streets and plazas rang with sullen iron shutters. Scores of curb stands sprouted everywhere, bright with bunting and flowers, to sell soft drinks, food, candles, pottery, mats, toys, and whirling *matracas,* or "bone busters," the noise of which was supposed to represent the breaking of the bones of Judas the Betrayer. The air was pungent with burned chili, hot hog fat, *tortillas,* and browning caramel. One procession began at eight at night and lasted until eleven—a thousand hymn-singing women carrying wax candles that flickered up and down the steep-hill streets like errant stars.

On the morning of Saturday of Glory hideous papier-mâché Judases were dangled by ropes above the multitude and then exploded with chain firecrackers. The crowd risked life and limb scrambling for the spilled contents—fruit, nuts, sugar cane, shoes, clothing, toys.

But the genial Christian spirit did not overtake the legislature. Its chief accomplishment after Holy Week was a law forbidding foreigners to engage in retail trade. This law was the worst "monster" ever to appear "in any legislative hall on earth," Steve commented. But the Fredonian revolt had seared Mexican hearts deep with hate.

In view of the unfavorable situation, Steve felt that he ought to accompany Mier y Terán on a trip to Mexico City, but he did not have the necessary $500 to go. More and more he felt himself pushing against dark, slippery shadows. Anti-American sentiment lurked in every corner of the government service: delays, silly obstructions, and unpleasant polite contempt. Revolutionary turnover of personnel made it necessary to fix up things over and over. Nothing seemed finally decided.

In spite of growing difficulties, Steve remained loyal to Mexico and its government, but at times he now permitted himself the luxury of conjecturing what a free, independent Texas would be like. How would it fit into the jigsaw of European and American nations?

Not wanting Texas overwhelmed by southern slavery, he continued to reject annexation to the United States. American laws might not suit Texas, so different in origin, culture, resources, and needs. But independence might work. Farms and industries would flourish. In confidential quarters he risked saying that, unless things were remedied promptly, Texas would have to become free.

To one Mexican friend he remarked prophetically that, however much he might be criticized and abused by Mexicans and his fellow Americans, "the credit of settling this fine country and laying the foundations for a new nation which at some future period will arise here cannot be taken away from me."

13 · The Brazos Riot

GREAT JOY AWAITED STEVE when he returned to Texas. The Perrys had come. Steve rushed to Davis Point.

Perry had carried out all Steve's requests for plants, uniforms, books, and supplies, forgetting not one thing.

"I guess I was a little touchy and worried about tearing up old roots," he apologized. "But now we are here, thanks to you."

Emily was expecting another baby, and Steve suggested that she go back with him to San Felipe where she would have better care. "We have good doctors there now, half a dozen of them."

But it was Steve who fell desperately ill. Emily moved to a neighbor's house to make room for a nurse. He hovered between life and death for more than a month and was not able to sit up for six weeks.

A few days after he was allowed out of bed, he rode to see Emily.

"Last night," he wrote Perry, "she was safely delivered of a fine son. I give you joy—all is doing well—what a host of boys you have!"

General Mier y Terán was visiting Bradburn at Anahuac that November. On a pad Steve wrote, "Positive—must see him!" and he scribbled a note to Perry that in a few days he would set out in his Dearborn wagon. But his hand shook violently, and he was unable to go.

Settlers were up in arms over Bradburn for his seizures of property and protection of runaway slaves. His treatment of shipping was particularly objectionable. He charged vessels triple tonnage. The little launch *Champion* had had to pay a total of $1,500 for putting into three ports. Captain Rhodes Fisher, who aimed to become a settler, wrote Steve of similar treatment. "God help us," he wrote, "there are many tracks into the lion's den but none come out of it."

Steve took the matter up with Mier y Terán by letter. The general wrote back, assuring him that illegal payments would be refunded. More than ever Steve was convinced that his own quiet methods plus his faith in the general were justified.

But a new customs official, with a deputy at Brazoria, began making himself obnoxious. Egoistic and ambitious, George Fisher was a Serbian adventurer and a naturalized American citizen who had drifted to Mexico in 1822.

For a time he had been hired as secretary by the San Felipe *ayuntamiento.* Soon that body accused him of falsely reporting slave and tobacco smuggling and plans for revolt in order to ingratiate himself with higher authorities. The *ayuntamiento* was doubly touchy because the reports contained much truth. The San Felipe authorities seized Fisher's baggage, recovered missing records, and then ran him out.

Mier y Terán appointed him port collector. Even for such a bustling, self-important person, Fisher's new post was a difficult one, and he did not make things easier for himself or anyone else. He had a grudge and enforced the most harassing regulations rigorously. The slightest difference between manifests and cargo brought confiscation and heavy fines. Just as Stephen was recovering, Fisher ordered all vessels to present themselves in Anahuac up the Trinity, 150 miles off course at a place inaccessible at high tide, at some seasons not at all.

When Bradburn suppressed the elected *ayuntamiento* at Liberty and set up his own stooge government in Anahuac, the colonists and Brazoria traders hated Bradburn and Fisher even more.

Not until December—Mier y Terán had left by then— was Steve able to get downstream to visit the Perrys and greet his cousin Henry Austin, who had settled at Peach Point. Steve had secured for him a tract there.

He had also set aside a sizable tract for Henry's sister, Mary Holley, who at last was coming to visit Texas. Now Mary had come out on the *Spica* from New Orleans to help Henry get his place shipshape for his family. The prospect of seeing her made up for the discomfort of Steve's hard trip to the coast in bad wet weather with an ugly norther blowing. He was not strong yet, and the ride down in the damp air made his whole face ache painfully.

Steve had never spent a happier Christmas. He was astonished at all that Henry had done in so short a time. He had put up a fine house with a puncheon floor—the Bolívar House—and had brought down the expensive furnishings of his New York home, which were mingled with white board tables and rawhide and deerskin chairs.

Henry had a lively poetic fancy, seasoned by experience in many parts of the world, wisdom, and good humor— qualities that were lacking in oversensitive, ever-complaining James Perry. His wife was a woman of warmth, brains, and culture, and Steve had never seen lovelier children. There were three boys and three girls, from little four-year-old Henry, who looked like a bright-cheeked wax doll, to beautiful Mary, who was sixteen.

Mary Holley proved to be as lively and intelligent as her letters to Steve over the years had led him to expect. For the Christmas party she sang a Brazos boat song she had composed and expected to publish. She loved dancing, so they had a gay time.

The season ended with Mary's departure on the *Spica* to return to New Orleans. "I'll be back soon," she promised.

She was never to set eyes on Texas again, but all her life she remembered Steve vividly as he had stood silhouetted against the early sun, waving good-by to her as the *Spica* slipped downstream. Eventually she published a volume of letters about her Texas experiences, a history of the region, and a brief account of Stephen's life and work.

Steve wrote that she had filled a great void because of the lack of congenial friends. "My sister's family and Henry's . . . and you, my friend, you—how shall I ever thank you for venturing into the wilderness; how to express the happiness of my ten days' visit at Henry's."

2

But not all was peace and good cheer on the lower Brazos that Christmas. A storm was brewing against Bradburn and Fisher. Hoping to avert trouble, Steve visited Colonel Domingo de Ugartechea in command of the Velasco garrison at the mouth of the river. The colonel's married sister in Saltillo had made Steve's stay there more pleasant.

In contrast to bull-necked Bradburn, the trim young officer was very much a gentleman. He refused to criticize his fellow officer or Fisher but admitted that the settlers had grievances and that the measures Steve proposed were wise.

"I shall try to calm the people down," Steve promised.

But time was running out. Wild talk grew wilder. Militarization of Texas, flouting of the civil authorities, arbitrary arrests by the soldiery, and harsh regulations on commerce made Brazoria seethe with threatening talk. "Bradburn is a puff adder," one businessman told Austin hotly. "Fisher is a slippery eel," said another. Ill feeling was stirred up still more by shady traders, smugglers, and various sea captains.

Steve urged calm. But right after Christmas, the *Boston Packet* and a smaller vessel, refused clearance by Fisher, forced their way to sea, firing on the guards and badly wounding one. The townspeople joined in the melee, and the excitement, Steve wrote, was "terrible." He had hard work to keep the settlers from marching on Anahuac and hanging Bradburn.

Steve wrote a harsh letter to the colonel:

Things in Texas are so critical great prudence is required by public officers especially of the military and revenue departments. Fisher's regulations are impracticable. . . . Their execution . . . impossible. . . . A flame is kindling that will remove the Guard from this river and reach . . . Anahuac and Mr. Fisher. . . . You know your native countrymen. . . . You also know that the people of Texas have many just causes for complaint. The country will be totally broken up and all commerce annihilated. Is that the object of the Government? Do the people of my colony merit being shut out from the whole world, their commerce destroyed? I think not.

So long as there was "a plausible hope" of avoiding "extremes," he was "opposed to bloodshed." "But if all honorable means of obtaining redress fails, we shall have to put our trust in ourselves, our rifles, and our God. . . . One word from me now would annihilate every Mexican soldier in Texas."

Aware that his letter might provoke military reprisals, Steve hurried back to his San Felipe headquarters, doing the 47 miles in one day and part of the night.

He found Emily dancing at a ball. Telling him that he was getting too solemn, she forced him to join in the fun. Guests had come from 50 miles about on horseback or in wagons. The fiddlers were aided by a player beating on a U-shaped whiffletree clevis with an iron pin. The dancers "shuffled" and "double-shuffled" and "wired" and "cut the pigeon's wing," making the splinters fly.

Bradburn, upon receiving Steve's letter, was amazingly conciliatory. Though it had been "a difficult" one for a person in his position to receive and had thrown him "into consternation," he suggested a personal meeting. Too tied up with public works at Anahuac to travel to San Felipe, he would gladly go part way, to San Jacinto or Buffalo Bayou.

They had a frank talk at Lynche's farm near the bayou. Steve admitted he had been overwrought but insisted that Fisher and his regulations had to go. Military force had to respect civil rights.

Bradburn made solemn promises. Steve thought him "a jackass," as he wrote Mary, but hoped for improvement.

Mier y Terán, reading a copy of Stephen's letter to Bradburn, flew off the handle. No customs officer, he wrote Steve, could have all his documents in two different places; yet he had been considerate enough to put a subordinate in Brazoria.

All the favors you have received from the government of Mexico and its agents have merely produced in you a capacity to form erroneous judgments and unjust complaints which cause discord and riots in the colonies. . . . If we have broken the laws, direct your complaints . . . to the government. But you are not authorized to indulge in either insolence or riots which I have the means to suppress. . . . You will see how far we can go. . . .

How dare you say . . . that the government wishes to destroy all commerce in your colony? [In all America] from Hudson Bay to Cape Horn, in what nation and in what port are duties not paid or do ships fail to visit the customs house? . . . Only in Brazoria are there complaints. . . . Only in Brazoria do boats go out secretly, firing like pirates, wounding a Mexican soldier. . . .

Is this the hospitality that a soldier in the service of Mexico finds in Señor Austin's colonies?

The Brazoria revenue guards, believing themselves among friends and loyal citizens, could have had their throats cut. If they are among enemies, they will act accordingly. The Mexican soldier has had enough experience to know "how to treat enemies."

Steve was worried. Lately people had been warning him that Mier y Terán hated all foreigners and planned to break Steve's power in Texas.

"That's idle talk," Steve had retorted. "Mier y Terán has always been friendly and cooperative."

But now Steve's hasty, disrespectful words had been given a treasonable meaning that was not intended. A powerful friend had perhaps been alienated.

Ignoring Mier y Terán's threats, Steve wrote back in friendly tenor, telling him exactly what had happened. He had been indiscreet but had seen no other way to stop worse violence. It would be a shame if so many years' toil in taming the wilderness and building up Texas were to be wiped out by a man of Fisher's stripe. Only his prompt removal would prevent more trouble.

But the Brazoria incident had inflamed all Mexico. Rancorous memories of the Fredonian revolt were given free rein. Rumors grew of wild revolt all over Texas. Steve was now a man marked by the ruling military caste of the country.

Events in Mexico and in Texas were moving fast toward new issues and new violences.

14 · Revolution

DURING STEVE'S LONG ILLNESS his desire to be free of colony affairs and to retire to a quiet farm life had grown stronger. He had spent his convalescence making plans for a large two-chimney plantation house that he and the Perrys would erect on the bay shore.

It would spread in two wings on either side of a wide, central hall with end doors surmounted by showy half-round fan windows. Ten stately cedar columns would support a wide front gallery, and all bedrooms would have porches or terraces for coolness and a view of Galveston Bay. Emily thought the plans were entirely too pretentious.

Then came the Brazoria trouble, and the governor testily ordered Steve to resume his seat in the legislature at once. "A fatiguing journey," he wrote Mary Holley, "attended perhaps with difficulties and dangers."

He did not get off until late March. With him he took his nephew Moses Austin Bryan, Emily's oldest boy, of whom he had grown very fond.

Moses was instantly a slave to beautiful black-eyed Ursula Veramendi, Jim Bowie's wife. Bowie had built a fine mansion out near the missions.

Don Erasmo and other friends were angry with Bowie for his loud independence talk. But Steve wished no feud with him. Jim had a hair-trigger temperament, and his land deals, his contacts with influential Mexicans, and his marrying into the richest clan in Texas made him a power.

Steve had brought along a colony memorial to the federal government asking for exemptions from the 1827 tariff, modification of the rigid 1830 colonization law, and land titles for East Texas settlers.

But the San Antonio *regidores,* already miffed at not having been consulted first, feared that to endorse it at such a ticklish time would be construed as revolt. The popular Santa Anna uprising against Bustamante was spreading. Aristocratic folk, like the Veramendis, feared any uprising of "the people" in behalf of the 1824 constitution. Don Erasmo, as stanchly republican as when Steve had first met him, favored Santa Anna. He succeeded in persuading the *ayuntamiento* to endorse Steve's proposals.

Though wild rumors of the Brazoria incident still circulated, Steve got along better with the Saltillo legislature than he had dared hope. It promptly supported the Texas memorial. So did the governor.

Alamán, Mier y Terán, and the president, too hard pressed to court any trouble, wrote him favoring his proposals, and the president agreed to lay them before Congress.

The duty-free provisions for Texas were extended two

years. Steve wished that tools, furniture, iron, and steel rather than whisky could be on the free list, but it was a great concession. Fisher was removed, and Steve wrote Sam jubilantly that Bradburn and Mier y Terán were not enemies of the colony. The settlers had "more to fear from the imprudence of drunks and talking demagogues among themselves than from the government." If there were no more violence in Brazoria and no more wild speeches, everything would work out well.

He realized now that the colonists had had no right to get mixed up in the customhouse dispute. "How silly and imprudent," he wrote cousin Mary ruefully, "the best of us will talk and act sometimes when under excitement."

He decided that he should have a personal conference with Mier y Terán in Tampico, especially as the general was being talked of as a compromise president.

Steve left Moses Bryan in Saltillo. The youth, he wrote Emily, already could speak Mexican and had a Mexican sweetheart.

2

Steve rode to Monterrey and across rolling hill country through blazing sun and whirling dust. In Linares he learned that the Santa Anna revolt had swept into Tamaulipas, forcing Mier y Terán to flee 60 miles inland to Hacienda del Cojo (Lame Man). There he issued a proclamation accusing the Santa Anna party of being merely the tool of foreigners.

Stephen exploded. "This will lose him the good opinion of all but fanatic fools and old Spaniards."

He rode along overgrown stony trails, a long hard trip, to Cojo. The general, sick and all but overwhelmed, claimed to be too busy to see Steve.

When he finally did, he said stubbornly that, as soon as he put down revolt, he would send Fisher back in as customs collector. In defeat he had become a stiff-necked militarist indeed.

But Steve explained things calmly, and the general thawed. Though swamped with work and worry, he talked with Steve every free moment.

He grudgingly agreed that the 1830 law needed changing, Texas should have more commercial rights, duties on many goods should be lifted, and special concessions should be given to the first settlers in slavery matters.

At their last meeting he embraced Steve warmly. "You and I are the only two men in the world who know how to settle Texas affairs."

Steve rode sadly out of Cojo wondering what would happen to General Mier y Terán, to the government, to Mexico, and to his own colony in the swirling storm of this revolution. Avoiding rebel lines, he cut down to the coast north of Tampico through jungle-fever country. He arrived exhausted in Matamoros at the mouth of the Rio Grande and wrote Sam:

These long trips in the sun through the wilderness, totally destitute of every comfort for the traveler, are truly wearisome to the body, to the health, to the patience and to the mind, but if I can do any good for the colony, I shall feel myself well compensated.

3

In Texas new abuses and arrests by Colonel Bradburn brought on an attack by armed settlers on his garrison in a new stone guardhouse at Anahuac. Other settlers stormed Fort Velasco at the mouth of the Brazos and captured it after eleven hours of bloody battle. Elsewhere in Mexico the Santa Anna revolt was unfolding fast in flame and battle. On June 8 rebels under the command of Colonel José Antonio Mexía, agent of the speculating Galveston land company, entered Matamoros on the brigantine *Santa Anna* and fired three warning shots. Most of the garrison shifted to Santa Anna's side and escorted Mexía in triumph to the plaza.

Everything, thought Steve, was carried out with remarkable good order, no violence, no looting, no confiscations. After only an hour's lull, merchants and townsfolk went about their usual business.

It was feared that Mier y Terán might attack with his whole army. Again Steve wrote his colonists to "take no part in the civil war."

But within five days the forces of Mier y Terán were trapped and cut to pieces, and Steve climbed on the Santa Anna band wagon. To the showy military leader he sent warm personal greetings.

"I would not be a lover of the fundamental principles of constitutional liberty . . . if I failed to respect the Chief whose arms have always been used to protect them." Steve argued for "constitutional democracy" and a free press in order to create a "united public opinion" to "beat down aristocratic privilege and abuse." Rumors of Texan revolt were utterly "false." The militarists had insulted the flag by trampling on the constitution which the settlers had loyally tried to protect.

Harassed by guerrillas, Mier y Terán moved his broken forces to Padilla. There, where Iturbide had been put before the firing squad, he plunged a sword through his body. Santa Anna, the new national hero, was now triumphant in all Tamaulipas as in most of the country.

Steve paid his respects to Colonel Mexía and thought him "a liberal and good man." As a member of the Mexican legation in Washington for ten years, he knew and understood Americans. But he was convinced that the Texans were scheming to secede from Mexico and was preparing to invade the province.

"Wholly unnecessary!" Steve told him. "There are no plans for secession. No sentiment favors it."

"That I shall see for myself," replied Mexía.

"The disturbance was due merely to arbitrary acts by the government and the military against the rights of Coahuila and Texas," Steve insisted.

Mexía refused to give up the expedition but invited Steve to accompany him.

To keep one foot in the door of the old guard, Steve wrote the acting governor that he could not resume his seat in the legislature because he was obliged to go with Mexía to Texas, although a sea voyage was always "injurious" to his health.

4

Mexía and Stephen Austin arrived at the mouth of the Brazos on July 16. The colonel threatened "drastic measures" unless he were assured that the recent trouble was in support of Santa Anna, in which case he would "unite with them to accomplish their wishes."

Steve tried to persuade all Texas to declare for the Santa Anna movement. Músquiz should "pronounce for Santa Anna and arrest those opposed"! Only such a step would guarantee peace. He sent similar appeals to Nacogdoches, La Bahía, and other places and to Sam Williams in San Felipe.

The strict neutrality that Stephen had long preached was gone. His repeated instructions to his colonists to avoid Mexican political struggles were wiped out. Sooner or later the people had to participate in the life of the country. Now, with revolutionary troops at their doors, their choice was not going to be in favor of the Bustamante government that had sent Bradburn and Fisher to pester them.

Alcalde John Austin headed a committee to welcome Mexía and Stephen Austin and present copies of resolutions adopted by the authorities, the volunteers, and the people.

"There was never the slightest intention to separate from the Mexican Confederation," he told Mexía. "The colonists are Mexicans by adoption and in their hearts remain so. We are farmers not soldiers, but since 1830 we have been governed by despotic militarism and have been driven to arms to keep abusive subalterns within limits. We did not attack the flag but sought to protect it against those who outraged it by using it as a pretext for encroachments upon the constitution and sovereignty of state and nation. For these reasons the inhabitants have united with General Santa Anna to procure peace under the shield of the constitution."

Mexía and Stephen were escorted to Brazoria and greeted by the thunder of twenty-one guns and vollies of musketry by the Velasco volunteers. *Regidor* William Wharton, although secretly a secessionist, gave the welcoming speech, and honor guards escorted them to dinner at John Austin's house. Music, bonfires, illuminations, and cannon and musketry firing continued all night. "Such rejoicing and enthusiasm I have never seen," Steve wrote. "Right or wrong we have to pull together."

A Santa Anna dinner-ball was arranged for the twenty-second. Steve would have preferred to have joined Mexía's troops and Johnson's volunteers to capture Anahuac and take "that jackass Bradburn."

After a few shots the garrison revolted in favor of Santa Anna, but Bradburn escaped through a secret exit from an underground powder magazine that slaves had constructed in the dark of the moon.

Hotly pursued, he galloped toward the Sabine and plunged into the river just above the ferry crossing. Bullets peppered about his head. On the United States side he struggled through steaming swamps for 8 miles on foot.

Convinced that Texas would not secede and that it would soon be freed of all Bustamante partisans, Mexía sailed his troops back to Matamoros.

5

Steve hurried to San Felipe. The new Santa Anna volunteer corps led him enthusiastically into the plaza where
the regular militia was drawn up. He was welcomed with
a twelve-round salute of cannons and small arms and with
speeches.

"Well done, good and faithful servant; thou art welcome,
thrice welcome, to thy home and friends!"

Steve urged "fidelity to the constitution of our adopted
country. Free democracy has reasserted its rights under
the banner of Santa Anna."

At Palmito Creek, Mexican troops, captured at Velasco
but now supporting Santa Anna, gave him another musketry salute. He embraced the Mexican officers amid
cheers: *"Viva la Federación! Viva la Constitución!"* He was
tendered a big banquet. Every Mexican state was toasted.
The constitution was toasted. Texas was toasted as an independent state of the Mexican Confederation. Texas and
Coahuila were toasted as a state which, once separated,
would be united. Stephen was toasted. Everybody was
toasted.

Steve moved swiftly to bring all Texas into line. The
colonel of the Tenochtitlan garrison to the north refused
to declare in favor of Santa Anna or provide weapons to
the colonists and was taken prisoner. The La Bahía commander refused to join the town authorities in favor of
Santa Anna and withdrew to San Antonio to avoid bloodshed.

Once more Steve wrote Músquiz to hasten to come out for Santa Anna or else all Texas would rise up.

Calling the colony militia together at Bowman's ranch, he sent an officer with an ultimatum to Piedras:

There are alarming rumors that the free expression of Nacogdoches had been suppressed by force and by threats of inciting the Indians. If the settlers are to be given to the savage knife, they will have to defend themselves.

After a bloody all-day battle with the townspeople, Piedras threw his supplies down the church well and slipped out.

Jim Bowie, who happened to be in Nacogdoches, raced out with twenty men and ambushed Piedras's advance patrol at the Angelina River crossing, whereupon Piedras's own men seized him and declared for Santa Anna. Bowie asked Stephen to hurry forward horses and supplies so that the force could get on to San Felipe.

Steve tersely ordered the commander of San Antonio to declare for Santa Anna forthwith. The latter replied that he had already done so in union with the civil authorities and the people. All Texas was now a Santa Anna stronghold.

The Texas colonists had learned to fight against the authorities and to settle their own affairs. The iron was now hot to present grievances and win reforms.

15 · The Sovereign People

EMILY SHOWERED STEVE with complaints. The climate was wet and unpleasant. The disorders had hurt business. Nothing was going well. They would never get ahead. "We should never have come to Texas."

Steve, swamped with work and plagued with difficulties, was distressed. He wrote her that things had turned out differently than he had expected. "But in the end the country cannot do otherwise than prosper. If you were satisfied, I would not be in the least discouraged."

Her discontent came when he was striving to keep the Firebrands from controlling a special citizens' convention. He wanted to block all wild, unreasonable demands. Few native-born Mexicans appeared, but fifty-eight delegates from sixteen districts in eastern Texas showed up.

He was easily elected president over Firebrander William Wharton, but the latter's aggressive resolution against the 1830 law was adopted. Jared E. Groce, the biggest plantation slaveowner, brought in a tariff resolution. Indian relations were discussed, and the militia was reorganized into six companies. A firm demand for statehood was made.

Firebrand secessionists, like Bowie, denounced the convention as a "milk and water" business.

Wharton was named to carry the convention resolutions to the state and national governments, and Austin was put at the head of the permanent Committee of Safety—for no one knew what turn the revolution might take. Local correspondence committees were to be set up by other centers.

Steve wrote far and wide to get opinions. A Pine Bluff settler on the Trinity wrote sourly that no dangers threatened the colony.

A farmer from the upper Sabine said that convention delegates should be paid. Away from home for twenty-seven days, he had spent fifty dollars and had lost a valuable horse. "Some people with the most property here never see even fifteen dollars the year round."

Political Chief Músquiz wrote sharply that, though the settlers had legitimate grievances, the San Felipe convention was in violation of existing state and federal laws. He threatened drastic punishment.

"How could the government presume to say that the people of Texas had violated the constitution?" demanded Steve. "The people have a constitutional right to assemble peaceably and represent their wants. Unless Texas takes measures of her own for her welfare, all will be lost. In revolutionary moments any measure that irritates is bad and any that soothes is good. The meeting had calmed impatient spirits."

He declined to present Músquiz's harsh statement to the colonists and resigned his Mexican army commission. The political chief ordered him to continue till he could find out what the regulations about resignations were.

Steve threw down the gauntlet, informing Músquiz that, though it was a troublesome journey over bad roads at a time when Indians were dangerous and his private business was in no shape to be neglected, he intended to visit all the main centers in Texas to get common action on the San Felipe resolutions.

If the old Mexican towns, like La Bahía (whose delegates had arrived too late) and San Antonio (which had declined to send delegates), were to lead in pushing states rights and if American and Mexican Texans stood together, the authorities would be less likely to fear a secession plot and there would be more chance of winning reforms.

La Bahía readily promised support. In San Antonio, Steve put up at Seguín's town house and had a long talk with Músquiz.

"The Political Chief," he wrote back to San Felipe, "has the best interests of Texas at heart. He deserves the colony's confidence."

The leading citizens, Don Erasmo, Commander Antonio Elosua, Veramendi, and others were anxious for separation from Coahuila.

To the *ayuntamiento* Steve proposed that the federal government be told that, if grievances were not met by April, Texas would organize its own state government. All his proposals were adopted except the time ultimatum. He had obtained full Texas unity. Mexicans and Americans would stand side by side for their rights.

2

He had not reckoned with the Firebrands. In his absence Mexican haters and secessionists called another convention, which they hoped to control. Sam Houston, the "Raven," sent to Texas on a secret mission by his friend President Andrew Jackson, also helped drum up the second, or Firebrand, convention.

The American government was putting pressure on Mexico to sell Texas, and Minister Anthony Butler boasted that his country would soon have Texas. The Mexican authorities were more frightened than ever, and Steve's efforts were undermined.

Some years before, following a scandalous separation from his wife, Houston had resigned as governor of Tennessee and had gone to live with the Cherokee in Arkansas near the Texas border. In his early youth he had run away from his widowed mother and her flock of small children to live with this tribe and had been adopted as the "Raven" because of his fierce black eyes and shiny black hair.

In Arkansas he took a pretty Indian consort, Tiana, and in their handsome wigwam he sired, some claim, at least one child. He made himself the leader of nearly all the Indian tribes west of the Mississippi. People claimed that he harbored a grandiose scheme to set up an independent Indian state from Arkansas to the Rockies. Others saw it as a plot to use the Indians to seize Texas. Sunk in drunken debauchery, Sam seemed too weak a reed for any such vast projects.

But in 1832 he sobered up, rebandaged the never-healed Indian wound in his shoulder, and headed east. In Tennessee he had his portrait painted as Marius in a Roman robe among ruined Roman columns, his chest and shoulder bare. In Washington, Jackson gave him funds, passport, and letters.

He kissed Tiana good-by for the last time. At the Texas border a crony gave him a razor. Houston, the story goes, boasted that someday it would "shave the chin of the president of a republic." As he splashed out of the muddy Red River upon the vacant Mexican plain of dirty red grass and jack oak, a prophetic eagle circled about his head.

He galloped down the Trammel Trace, now worn deep by American settlers. In Nacogdoches he saw interesting people and started a new affair of the heart. At planter Jared Groce's place, he held a secret consultation on Texas. He reached San Felipe on Christmas Day.

Houston and Bowie journeyed to San Antonio, where they put up at the Veramendi home. Houston was feted by leading citizens, but the authorities, believing he was a Jackson agent, were suspicious of his long lonely rides into Indian country. Was he scheming to use the Indians against Mexico?

The "official" ends "contemplated" by those Indian negotiations were "accomplished," remarked Houston. But the Secretary of War of the United States refused to pay his $3,500 expense account.

Finally Houston headed back for the United States. He saw Austin briefly in San Felipe. Their temperaments clashed. Irked by Sam's cocksureness as to what was best for Texas, Austin was reserved.

"Everybody wants independence," declared Sam, "and the Texans can lick the Mexicans any day. They have already done it."

"Why should the Texans, who are Mexican citizens, fight Mexico?" asked Steve. "The majority of hard-working settlers want justice; they want statehood. If Texas were part of the United States, its cotton would have to compete with cotton in half a dozen states. As part of Mexico, Texas has a big privileged market. Our friend Jared Groce should be the first to know that."

Houston was aware then that Austin knew what was going on in the colony.

Houston said he was setting up in Nacogdoches to practice law. "From now on Texas will be my permanent home, and I'll be back for the convention," he warned. "We'll see what the settlers really want."

"I'll go along with whatever the majority decides," said Steve stiffly.

Houston, a brilliant lawyer and student, was a romantic symbol of the lawlessness and the force of the lusty frontier. Steve, though he had led the first frontier rush into Texas, was a symbol of work and law. Sam's dashing self-important manner and his demagoguery grated on Steve. Sam could not stomach Steve's puritanism. From this time on, he sneeringly referred to him as "the little gentleman."

Sam hurried to Natchitoches, off Mexican soil, to write President Jackson that all his information favored the President's views concerning the acquisition of Texas by the United States. Nineteen-twentieths of the population desired this.

Actually none of the Mexicans wanted it. Most American settlers were still opposed to commotion and war.

Houston promised to keep Jackson informed of the course adopted at the Texas convention. He believed that a state government would be set up that would "remain separate from the Confederacy of Mexico. She has already . . . repelled all the troops of Mexico from her soil. [This was not remotely true.] She can defend herself against the whole power of Mexico. . . ."

Steve realized that the extremist convention called behind his back would alienate La Bahía and San Antonio, whose cooperation he had just won. The Firebrands, playing on race hatred to feather their own nests, to discredit Austin, and to gain political control, soon whipped up such feeling that anyone who said a good word for Mexicans was in physical danger.

Músquiz warned that this gathering would also be illegal and advised the governor at Saltillo that the colonists were aiming, not at statehood, but full independence.

3

In the midst of Steve's worries, Emily continued to complain even though he had turned over to her and Perry part of his prized Peach Point tract on the Brazos River. They had built a log house there and had moved into it in January.

Steve hoped that they were happy in their new home. He reminded them, on sending Perry the deed to the property, that his own situation was not rosy. He desperately needed several thousand dollars to pay an old debt and to get through the fall.

I certainly think your removal to Texas will make your children all independent. This never would have been possible in Missouri. I am surprised that you say we shall never live to realize anything from my labors—Is it nothing to have paid nearly all the old debts—to have given credit to the name of my family by settling this colony that will be permanent and honorable for ages to come—Is it nothing that you are now permanently settled with the certainty your children will not enter the world penniless? . . . You let trifles have too much influence on you. . . . If I had the power of a magician to build palaces, I would not do it.

Local and national affairs moved dramatically on. In March, Santa Anna had himself chosen president by sixteen of the nineteen states. Mexía, now a senator, reminded Steve that he had been promised land in the colony. Austin should head a Texas commission to Santa Anna's inauguration on April 1. "A public testimony of this nature would be of great convenience to all interested."

But on April 1 the Firebrand convention met. Santa Anna, instead of taking office, told Vice-President Valentín Gómez Farías to run the government and slipped off to his estate in Veracruz.

Of the fifty-three convention delegates only fourteen had served previously. The Firebrands packed it, and Bill Wharton was chosen president.

Stephen told the assemblage that he had no wish to impose his own will on proceedings.

The situation of Texas is alarming. Anarchy and confusion threaten to close forever over the wreck of the Mexican Republic. Bloody civil war still rages in every corner—brother contending with brother in deadly strife. The constitution, the instrument we have been taught to look upon as the sacred charter of our liberties, is being violated and the military are now in full control. In Saltillo a corrupt mob, a mortifying spectacle, has intimidated the legislature into adopting measures insulting and injurious to Texas. The time has come to organize a separate government.

A new statehood resolution was drawn up by the lawyer and Galveston land agent, David G. Burnet, and a provisional constitution was adopted, largely a Spanish translation of the Massachusetts constitution of 1780 which happened to be at hand. Houston pushed through a resolution that Indian lands be protected against white encroachment.

Though the Firebrand party, determined on independence, was now in control, Austin's voice carried weight. The previous resolution concerning the 1830 law was made more respectful. Immigration, industries, and trade were discussed. Surprisingly, since well-to-do settlers were slaveowners, a strong resolution against "inhuman and unprincipled traffic" in slaves was adopted.

Stephen Austin, Dr. James B. Miller, and Erasmo Seguín, who was not present, were chosen to carry the resolutions to the federal government.

4

Neither Miller nor Seguín could leave, and Steve, whose health was bad, dreaded the long, hard, costly trip alone.

He could ill afford to neglect his business. To Mary Holley he wrote:

Before this, I fully expected to have been settled on my own farm quite snug and comfortable. Instead . . . I am on the way for 1,200 miles on a mule's back . . . over plains and mountains to the City of Mexico, further from my hopes of farm and home than . . . ever. . . .

I am convinced we cannot do without a state government any longer. If we cannot get it peaceably, I shall unite with the hottest to get one by other means. If we are to have war, we must all go together but I hope that calamity will never fall on Texas.

He foresaw great personal danger, maybe death. He wrote Emily and Perry that, when he returned, he would "get a wife and be a farmer," but if he never came back, his will was in his desk. He sent a record of money owed him. His swords and personal mementos should be saved for the children. The tomahawk that his father had used on his first trip to Texas was to be passed on to Stephen, his nephew. "I . . . also carried it on most of my exploring trips. . . . It has blazed the way for North Americans to Texas." He made suggestions for the education of all the children and sent down several horses as gifts.

"It is a great sacrifice to go," he remarked, "but if I get the 1830 law repealed, I will be satisfied. If not I will have lost time, money, health, and will be repaid with only abuse. The Sovereign People are the hardest masters on earth."

Trouble developed even before he shoved off. Mexía wrote that George Fisher had been ordered back to the customs post. Steve angrily got the appointment blocked.

Fisher accused him of persecuting his wife and children, who were penniless in Texas, and threatened him and the colony with dire revenge.

Asiatic cholera hit the mouth of the river. At first it spared younger children, but by April 16 there were already seven adult deaths. "Dreadful!" Stephen wrote the Perrys. "How I tremble for you all!"

16 · Mission to Mexico

DELAYED BY DRIVING RAIN and high waters, Steve reached San Antonio on April 29. He reported to Músquiz on the cholera epidemic and asked prominent citizens to meet with him.

A new harsh law forbade *ayuntamientos* or more than three people to sign petitions. The San Antonians were sullen at the independent action of the North American colonists and were afraid to sign the new petition. Only Seguín supported Steve wholeheartedly.

Stephen traveled on alone to La Bahía, which also turned a deaf ear to his appeals, and headed for Matamoros to talk with Commandant Vicente Filisola.

Steve did not know that his friend Músquiz had rushed to Saltillo to denounce his efforts or that the acting political chief was dynamiting his trail behind and ahead. The La Bahía citizens were warned that San Antonio had repudiated Austin, not to be fooled by him. The chief ordered San Felipe and other towns to retract their stand or suffer castigation. One by one they did. He warned General Filisola that Austin had been "agitating" and that his petitions were in violation of the law.

The general, believing all Texas in revolt, was preparing an armed expedition and refused to see Steve. Too weak from dysentery and cholera to stand, Steve toiled over repeated messages to him. The convention was not "revolt." Elected by the majority of the people as their commissioner, he had come here to inform the general of the truth about Texas. The colony now produced 70,000 arrobas of cotton, had thirty ginning mills, two sawmills, and water and flour mills. It was ready for statehood.

Filisola did not answer for a week. Though admitting that Steve's proposed reforms were reasonable, he condemned the "illegal" convention harshly.

Steve replied that the constitution gave the colonists the right to petition. "A federal republic cannot exist without free discussion." He sent copies of the resolutions and requested that Filisola forward them to the top Mexican officials so that they would know Texas was not in revolt and what reforms were desired.

Reluctantly Filisola received Steve. The general struck him as "blunt, honest and candid, a prompt soldier." An old-school reactionary officer, in thirty years of unusually distinguished public service he had never enriched himself by graft.

He complained to Steve of the smuggling of tobacco and slaves by the colonists. "My reports say that the steps taken in Texas have not been conducive to tranquillity. I am told you have been stirring up trouble to get Texas to secede."

"That is utterly false." Steve explained the situation.

"It has been reported to me that several United States generals in disguise are in Texas inflaming the people," continued the general.

Steve lifted one eye quizzically. "I would be the first to know about anything like that. If the reforms Texas desires are granted, any Firebrands among us will have little influence."

"But you and other Americans——"

Steve broke in sharply. "I am a Mexican citizen and as loyal as you or any other citizen. Not a hairbreadth of Mexican territory is in danger. For ten years we have begged to be given local courts. Coahuila has never listened. The federal government has never listened. Statehood will give us such reforms at once."

The general was not unalterably opposed to statehood, but he was ordering all garrisons re-established. With a cold smile he added, "The Galveston customhouse will be reopened under George Fisher. He is already here in Matamoros."

The Serbian had filled the general's ear with evil reports, but it was not the time to make it an issue. Instead Steve called on Fisher.

They got along better than he had hoped. Fisher seemed pathetically eager to avoid new difficulties. He claimed that Bradburn had obliged him to enforce regulations little to his taste. The violence in Brazoria had been egged on by smugglers, sea captains, and illicit traders.

Steve promised to inform the settlers of these facts and to urge them to give Fisher full support. The hatchet was buried.

Steve wrote Sam Williams, "A dark squall that seemed gathering when I arrived, I have not seen lately."

General Filisola was reluctant to let Steve go on to Mexico City. "Congress will have adjourned before you arrive. Would it not be better to wait here till you find out how the government reacts to your petitions?"

Steve walked along the water front, considering the general's menacing suggestion that he abandon his mission.

Still sick with dysentery, he was in no condition to make a hard trip on which he might perish from fever or assassination. Steve was sorely tempted to return to Texas to recover his health and await results. But would the general forward his petitions? Would any results be obtained unless Steve pushed matters personally?

A large vessel was putting off on the morrow. It would reach Veracruz in a week, which would be better than a month of rough horseback riding even though Steve always got deathly seasick.

Filisola urged him more pointedly not to go.

"I have been commissioned to go. I must go," Steve told him.

With bad grace Filisola visaed his passport to depart.

2

Steve staggered on deck. The trip had been wretched because of bad weather and a leaky boat. There had been a whole month, not a week, of deathly seasickness, salty provisions, and only a few sips of water a day.

Beyond the black-and-red island of San Juan de Ulúa, church towers and public buildings poked out of the hot, silver haze above the low, white, sandy coast. The wharf was crowded with colorful townsfolk: peons with bright serapes or cotton *rebozos* and wealthy men in double pantaloons with lace or embroidery inserts in side slits and big, dark hats laced with silver cord.

The port commandant, General Ciraco Vásquez, sternly forbade Steve to leave for the capital. Steve knew then that he was a marked man. But he was carrying the people's message, and before his honest pleas for justice, even the most stupid officials would have to give ground. Indeed, the next morning, with a sly smile under tallow lids, Vásquez told Steve that he could proceed to Mexico City.

The hotel attendant knocked on Steve's door at 2 A.M. A boxlike vehicle, decorated with cherubim and clouds and drawn by four mules, passed through the dark, cobbled streets and the city gates and plowed through sand under palm and coconut trees, masses of tangled vines, and scarlet flowers. Indian women, wrapped in bright skirts, torsos bare save for draped red kerchiefs, stood at doorways with naked babies in their brown arms. Venders offered hot cinnamon chocolate or cool fruit drinks and tamales in shiny banana leaves.

The mules were changed at pleasant bamboo and thatched villages, which were set in gardenlike vegetation. Soon cavalry in blue coats and scarlet pants escorted them, red pennants flying from long glistening lances.

Among the orange and lemon groves in the rolling foothills above the tierra caliente, the air grew cooler. They stopped for dinner at twilight and set out again at midnight, lurching through blackness over terrible ruts till a half moon bathed the rustling vegetation and the slim Orizaba snow peak needled the sky. As dawn creamed over high white mountains, they rolled into dew-drenched Jalapa and traveled along steep, cobbled streets above sharp jungle ravines.

Here Austin was placed under arrest in the guardhouse, charged with not having had his passport stamped by the Veracruz commandant. General Vásquez had played him a dirty trick. Only after several days did Steve secure permission to appeal to the Minister of Relations to be taken to the capital to recover his shattered health and complete his mission. But not for many days did orders come to release him.

The stage rolled out of Jalapa behind eight white horses and struggled up steep ravines to the black lava tablelands. The next day, starting before daybreak, they crossed barren plains, rugged country growing drearier and colder, where only an occasional, forlorn straw hut was seen among the lava rocks. Long lines of mule drivers in big hats and red sashes carried goods to the coast.

But on the rich, green Puebla plain, smiling under the sun, was spread out the great "City of the Angels," shiny with the domes of tiled churches. Along the lofty flanks of magnificent Iztaccihuatl, the "White Woman," glaciers flashed violet in the dazzling sun. Cavalry escorted them through bandit-infested Río Frío—"Cold River"—and the Black Forest. Brakes squealing, they rolled downhill for hours and then swung along the edge of a mighty cliff.

Again Steve looked down upon Mexico City, its tall towers among gleaming lakes and green plains, this time from the same point that three centuries earlier the conqueror Hernán Cortés had gazed upon the great Aztec lake and its great carved temples and gaily decorated boats.

17 · End of a Dream

In Mexico City, Steve put up at Henry Offut's Hotel Washington. Board and room cost him sixteen pesos a week. He smoked a cigar with each meal and once a day took a glass of brandy or a "mint sling." Occasionally he bought a bottle of Madeira.

Steve called on Valentín Gómez Farías, the acting president, to explain his mission. Their talk was brief and stiff, but to the colony Steve wrote favorably of the vice-president's efforts to curb army and church. Texas had little good to expect from either institution. The country would long "remember Gómez Farías with gratitude."

Steve also called on all the cabinet ministers to urge statehood and reforms and followed up with repeated memorandums.

Congress was bitterly opposed to statehood for Texas. A strong clique, scheming for a big land-grab, wished to make it a territory. This solution was favored by Gómez Farías and by representatives of the Galveston land company. That concern's chief Texas agent was now General John Mason, who formerly had come to Texas to try to pry $30,000 out of Steve for the Hawkins estate.

In and out of the intrigue threaded Minister Anthony Butler, who had big personal interests in Texas. Scheming for annexation, he wrote a secret report to Washington that Austin's ideas of "fidelity to Mexico" and his influence with Texans made him America's worst foe in getting hold of Texas.

Steve fought the territorial party tooth and nail and beat it. He made many powerful enemies, among them the acting president.

Again Steve called on him to urge statehood. He insisted that the settlers were loyal to Mexico. The injustices they were suffering could be cured only by self-government. If Texans were not granted reforms, the people would certainly set up their own state government. Gómez Farías took this as a threat and ordered Steve from his presence.

Quite out of patience, Steve penned a strong letter to the San Antonio *ayuntamiento*, telling it that, if Texas did not "take all its affairs" into its own hands, it would be "lost." This defiant, indiscreet message was to change Steve's fate and alter the destinies of Texas, Mexico, and the United States. It was to shake the whole continent.

Cooling off, the next day he wrote Gómez Farías courteously that he had made no threat. He had merely stated a fact. Forcefully he reiterated all the Texan claims.

Steve was also upset by news that sorehead colonists

were accusing him of every crime on the calendar. He denounced the "poor devils, brutal and ungenerous, all the rough boys who hated Mexicans." Only a "fool would keep on serving such people. . . . Let others take the lead. . . . In the future I will look after my own comfort."

Actually wilder Texans were not clamoring for anything just then, for crops had been bad, Indian raids had occurred, and cholera was sweeping the whole colony.

Emily had miraculously recovered, but her youngest child by Bryan was dead. Moses Bryan, now in San Antonio, had escaped. John Austin of Brazoria, his wife, and children were gone. Henry Austin lost his wife and lovely Mary. He sent the other children to Mary Holley. "A great vacuum has been left," wrote Perry. "An unusual frost has allayed the disease, and corpses are gradually being burned." His cotton and that of all the settlers had been ruined. Pumpkins and some corn were doing well, but there was no one to harvest them. Cholera had taken its biggest toll among the Negro cabins.

News of other losses came through. Death had ridden down the Veramendis and Ursula at Monclova, where they had fled to escape the cholera raging in San Antonio. All had died. Grieving for his wife, big Jim Bowie had returned from Louisiana with his huge Negro body servant to drown his desperate sorrow in the grogshops.

Steve was brightened by getting the 1830 law amended in spite of bitter opposition.

"The delay due to cholera," he wrote home, "has done no harm. It has aided better understanding. There is nothing like patience and perseverance."

That other eternal Mexican plague, revolution, was also

coming to an end. After a hard campaign President Santa Anna crushed the last rebels against the church reforms and entered Mexico City triumphantly at the head of a huge military parade to take back the reins of office from Gómez Farías.

Steve was glad for the change and arranged an interview with the new chief.

Santa Anna seemed far different from public accounts, not flamboyant, but quietly dressed and gentlemanly. His melancholy black eyes in his thin sallow face gave him a sad, humble expression. Steve reminded him of his letter of adhesion from Matamoros and of all he had done to get Texan support for his revolutionary movement.

The president said suavely that he was not sure about statehood and that the immigration question needed more study but promised that Texas should have special consideration. He called a cabinet meeting in order that Austin could present his arguments.

Santa Anna promised to lift immigration restrictions for a trial period of six months, to aid colonization and postal service, and to back a law for local courts and trial by jury. Steve was thoroughly convinced that Santa Anna was a true friend of Texas.

But on December 10, pleading illness, the president abruptly handed his office back to Gómez Farías. All his promises to Steve, except the easing of the immigration regulations, were blown to the winds.

Having little hope of accomplishing more in the face of Gómez Farías's ill will, Steve decided to travel north with the new Northwest commandant, General Pedro Lemus.

As a final good-will gesture, he called on Gómez Farías.

Steve admitted that he had been impatient, perhaps because of ill health. The antichurch reformer said graciously that he was convinced Austin had only the best interests of Texas at heart and was not seeking annexation to the United States. They embraced warmly as good friends.

2

Not able to leave as soon as Lemus, Steve traveled with friends in the coach of a congressman. Though they pushed ahead fast for nearly a week, they were unable to catch up with the general.

Saying good-by to his friends, Steve dashed on by horse, doing as much as 60 miles in one day, but did not catch up with Lemus until Saltillo, more than two weeks after leaving Mexico City. He was thoroughly worn out.

General Lemus informed him almost apologetically that he had just received orders from the Mexican War Department to arrest him and send him back to Mexico City.

"This will inflame all Texas," Steve warned him.

"Someone has blundered. You have good friends, in Mexico City; this will be straightened out quickly."

"My only crime has been to tell the government what Texas needs. Before you send me back, let me calm down the colonists."

To this Lemus agreed.

3

Steve advised the colonists that any excitement over his arrest would not help him or Texas.

"Do not endorse any revolutionary measures. . . . Let me perish if such is my fate."

To his family he was not so serene.

Ever since I returned from San Antonio to find a convention called in my absence, I have been suspended over the altar of sacrifice. I should never have compromised with the little clique of Mexican haters. I should have told them: "Texans, you must harmonize with San Antonio and Bahía—with the Mexican population." The oldest Mexican Texas settlements deserved that much respect and deference. I expect to be hammered and pummeled for a whole year, but believe good will come of it for Texas.

To Rafael Llanos, Senator from Nuevo León, a friend since 1821, who had helped promote Steve's ideas for the constitution of 1824, he poured out all his hopes for Texas —his efforts, tribulations, dreams.

Was it a crime for me to have spent thirteen years in a life of weariness, peopling the wilderness? I have been accused of having magnificent schemes for Texas, and I confess I have had them. It was depopulated; I wished to people it. The population was backward. I wished it advanced and improved by the introduction of industrious farmers, liberal republicans. I wanted the savage Indians subdued, the frontier protected, the lands cultivated, roads and canals opened, river navigation developed, and the rivers covered with boats. Such were some of my magnificent, and, as it now appears, visionary plans, but any Mexican not sharing them is scarcely a patriot. A moral revolution is required to overthrow the Gothic politico-religious system set up by Rome and Spain to hold the people in subjection like beasts of burden. If Mexico won't right Texas grievances, she ought to sell the province to the United States so as to get some profit from it before losing it.

He wrote Seguín sadly that he had entered Texas in 1821 "in the flower of my life, an enthusiastic philanthropist. Now, at the age of forty, I find myself . . . tired of men and their affairs."

Moses Austin Bryan wrote home from San Antonio that his uncle's arrest for treason had caused great excitement. "I am fearful it will go hard with him."

18 · Stone Walls

STEVE LAY ON THE COLD stone slab in his cell reading a French translation of Plato's *Republic*.

Few sounds penetrated. Only with his ear close to the double iron doors could Steve hear the footsteps of sentries. Several times he heard distant cannon salutes. If the wind were right, he could faintly hear the bugle on the roof sound reveille. The dim light through the tiny, smudged, iron-barred skylight high over his head, his only glimpse of the outside world, was barely enough for reading from ten to three on fair days. At night he had only a candle.

Several days each week he was taken to a sunroom on the roof for a half to two hours but was not allowed to speak to other prisoners. During the first weeks of imprisonment, an officer appointed to defend him had appeared briefly on three occasions and then was never heard of again. The only human he knew was his guard.

Steve recalled the chill clear to his heart, after the long trip back to Mexico under guard, when he was brought

149

here, February 13, to the Inquisition chambers: the screech of the big key in the outer iron gate at the corner of Santa Domingo Street, the diagonal walk through the long, black, vaulted corridor into the bowels of the establishment, the unlocking of the double iron doors of his cell.

Father Muldoon brought Steve's first ray from the outside. They embraced warmly, but they were allowed to talk only in Spanish in the presence of the prison commandant. The priest and Stephen's personal agent, William S. Parott, had tried to arrange bail. "It was blocked by Gómez Farías. That priest hater was the one who had you arrested."

"That can't be!" exclaimed Stephen. "We parted good friends."

"For all his noble words that man has a petty, spiteful streak. He would let you rot here before he would lift one finger or let anybody help you."

"But why am I held?"

"No one seems to know."

"What a system of jurisprudence!" exclaimed Steve. "If I do not know of what I am accused, how can I prepare my defense?"

"Even if you knew the charges, they would not permit you to secure evidence."

"What justice or common sense is that?" stormed Steve.

"I have heard talk about a letter that you wrote to the San Antonio *ayuntamiento*. They hint of treason."

"Tyrants, abusing their country, always accuse lovers of liberty of sedition and treason."

Muldoon persuaded the commandant to allow meals to be brought in, and Steve gave the priest an order on Parott for $200. The commandant's eyes flickered greedily. It was enough to provide good meals, with wine and cheese, for more than half a year.

Muldoon also promised to send books, but none came. Weeks went by, and time dragged heavily.

Finishing his meal, Steve looked up at the crude drawings of snakes and landscapes made by some prisoner of the Inquisition a century before and thought, "I prefer bread and water with books to the best eating without them. In a dungeon the mind and thoughts require aliment more than the body does."

It would seem that Muldoon, so intimate a friend of powerful Santa Anna, might have done more. The priest had gone to live with him on his Veracruz hacienda, but Steve's iron doors remained clanged shut, no visitors, no word, no books, no paper, no pen—nothing—just long, dim-skylight days, the guttering candle at night, the four bare walls.

Steve went over his ideas for Texas and made lengthy speeches to an imaginary convention about the need for roads and improvements. On some days the tedium was broken by earthquakes. Suppose the walls shook apart. What would the guards and prisoners do?

For a dollar he bought from his guard a small, soiled English book entitled *Yes or No*. It held no interest. One day Stephen got hold of the biography of Philip II in French and devoured it all day—the story of a monster who had had his own son killed by the Inquisition.

"Even a lion protects its young," noted Stephen, and he declaimed to his prison walls, "Mexico! Can you throw a glance at the history of Rome without feeling a pity for your ancestors and without shaking off at once the religious yoke which holds you enslaved? Can you contemplate the Inquisition without shuddering at the past and making an effort in favor of religious toleration so that ye may secure your liberties and safety for the future?"

The next day he walked for half an hour in the courtyard. "This," his guard said, "is where they buried the heretics."

"Assassinated in the name of religion!" exclaimed Steve. "It has been the same in all nations for all religions."

"Each of these dungeons has some tradition of the sufferings of some victim of the Inquisition or of the revolution," said his guard. "In that second-story cell, a Guatemalan was confined for thirty years. The great independence leader, General José María Morelos, was taken from that cell to be shot."

"At least," mused Steve, "my face is not covered with a mask. In Inquisition days prisoners' identities were kept unknown even to their guards."

On March 20 meals from the Washington Hotel ceased, and Steve was reduced to the stinking prison fare. The $200 given Muldoon had lasted less than a month. A sergeant demanded a "loan" of thirty dollars for the prison commandant. Steve forked over and hopefully paid ten dollars extra to have a note taken to Victor Blanco, a friend from Saltillo, asking him for books and pocket money.

Blanco sent him eighteen dollars and two days later a volume on Prometheus, a long, boring philosophical treatise. On the flyleaf were the words, "Cheer up, my beloved friend. We are all busy in your behalf."

2

A violent change came in Mexican politics. His confidence in Gómez Farías's antichurch policies undermined, Santa Anna returned to Mexico City accompanied by Muldoon to take back the reins of power. He turned wholly to the Church party, the army, and reaction. Gómez Farías had to flee for his life to New Orleans.

Father Muldoon came to see Steve again on April 29. He arranged his release from solitary confinement and said that Santa Anna had promised to free him by decree within a few days.

Steve's cell doors were left open from sunrise to 9 P.M. He had free use of the patio. Via a dark passage and stone staircase, he could visit second-story dungeons and mingle freely with other prisoners. All were men of standing, political leaders, officers, and priests. In the name of reform and the people, Gómez Farías had jailed thousands from all over the country.

Steve was allowed to write a monthly letter. "My confinement has been very rigid," he told Perry, "but I am in good health and have born it with tolerable patience."

Victor Blanco and Muldoon had been "firm and unwavering" in their friendship. Ramón Músquiz and others in San Antonio and on the Brazos had written in his behalf.

Though aware of Gómez Farías's malevolence, Steve wrote mildly that the exiled vice-president had been deceived into believing that he wished to deliver Texas to the United States. "A great absurdity! . . . I have no idea how long I will be held, but if my sufferings bring substantial good for Texas I will be content."

His arrest had already set things in motion. A member of Santa Anna's personal staff had been sent north to Texas to investigate. Other relief was obtained. New laws gave Texas trial by jury, judges, and a more generous land and immigration system.

"Every evil complained of has been remedied," wrote Steve. "This fully compensates me for all I have suffered."

Steve thanked the colonists for their calm but not for their indifference and complained to the Texas representative at the state capital:

A mild . . . respectful representation of the facts from the *ayuntamientos* of Texas . . . especially from San Antonio would open my dungeon at any time. . . . Perhaps this is too much to be done for S. F. Austin. . . . I did not think I was doing too much for those people when I risked everything. Likely I shall linger on here for years.

Not till June 15 did the military decide that it had no jurisdiction and delivered Steve to the civil prison, La Acordada, a miserable old building. But he was better treated, and visitors were allowed. Among those who came were Blanco, Miguel Ramos Arizpe, Parott, and Lucas Alamán, the great proclerical leader. Steve wished that Alamán were back at the head of the cabinet. "But he is too civilized and honest for Mexican political taste," he told a friend.

Not till July 11 did the court rule that it had no jurisdiction. The matter then slept on in the Supreme Court. After six months in prison, Steve still did not know either the charges or what court would try him.

Delayed letters came from Perry. Steve wrote back that he was delighted that the children were going to school.

Perry was to sell any of his property necessary to carry on their education. "I am now in tolerable health but have suffered . . . much rheumatism . . . the effects of the first years of settlement and of the damp air of the dungeon and want of exercise."

His case traveled from court to court, and Steve had to draw heavily to pay the lawyers' fees. "It has been reported I have millions in the banks of the United States. . . . $50,000 would set me in liberty. All I have on earth would not bring that sum, nor half of it."

Eventually the Supreme Court ruled that the Mexico City federal judge, Martínez de Castro, had to handle it.

Martínez is honest, but what can a foreigner and North American by birth, shut up in prison, almost destitute of friends and money, far removed from all resources, in the power of enemies, with the Minister of Relations at their head, reasonably expect except . . . perhaps total ruin?

Not till he was transferred to the city jail, the horribly dank, stinking Carcel de Belén, for questioning, did he learn what specific charges were contemplated.

The intention is to convict me of a design to separate Texas from Mexico and unite it to the United States. This is utterly false. All Texas can acquit me. I have been much more faithful to the government of my adopted country than my own welfare required. In place of imprisonment I deserve rewards from the government.

My innocence will not save me. The case can be prolonged without charges or any trial for at least six months more. After that I may have to send to Texas for proofs.

Friend Llanos, to whom he had written when arrested,

had treacherously turned his frank letter over to the authorities.

> But men of sense [Steve wrote] agree that my opinions therein and those of my indiscrete October 2 letter to the San Antonio *Ayuntamiento* are true and well-founded, not criminal. Unfortunately such blunt frankness is not to Mexican taste. I have been taught to speak the truth from infancy and am too old now to learn new habits.

By October he had sunk into deepest gloom, tinged with self-pity and resentment. To friends he wrote that they might as well look upon him as dead. To Sam Williams he wrote, "I expect to die in this prison. . . . I have no reason to make any other calculation." He had made "the fortunes of others" by distributing "millions of acres," but he feared he would have "to depend on Charity for six feet of ground to sleep in at rest."

A web he could not understand was woven around him.

19 · The Grand Conspiracy

THE FORCES AGAINST STEPHEN AUSTIN were powerful, so powerful that an influential friend close to the American Secretary of State wrote Steve he would be lucky if he were not wholly crushed. "There is a scheme to ruin you completely and strip you of all your influence and property."

In large part Steve blamed Minister Anthony Butler, who was leagued with powerful land-grabbers wishing Texas annexed to the United States. He charged that Butler was using secret propaganda "to arouse the people of Texas into rebellion" and "throw suspicion on me and perpetuate my imprisonment." He believes that the people there can be made "tools to promote the personal aggrandizement of Anthony Butler."

The ambassador also tried to sow suspicion between Steve and Williams.

"Is it not strange," Steve wrote Sam, "that the only man in Mexico . . . not anxious for my complete liberation should be the representative of my native country?"

Sam said he hoped they would "have the old dog in Texas someday—and give him his dues here."

While in prison Austin had had the last of his debt paid to Butler, but the American minister, though accepting the money, refused to turn over the final note to Steve's agent. "I have never in all my life known so bad and so base a man," Steve commented.

Other rancid hates were stirring. American hater Noriega, Mier y Terán's secretary, was telling investigators and the public that Austin ought to be shot for treason. Colonel Bradburn was testifying that Steve had collected arms for revolt.

Plotting elements in the Texas colonies, all the Mexican haters, all those scheming for annexation, official secret agents, and such were against Steve. The Wharton brothers assailed him in their rabid Brazoria paper *The Advocate of the People's Rights*. When Steve complained, William H. Wharton put out a handbill declaring:

> I pledge myself that when this bearer of instructions, this man of so many personal friends, this disinterested benefactor of Texas, this oracular weathercock . . . this turncoat victim, this maker of mottos, this organizer of parties, this presumptious dictator, returns, to brand him on the forehead with a mark that shall outlast his epitaph.

Sam Houston endorsed Wharton's attack. "It left the little gentleman very few crumbs of comfort."

Houston, agent for the Nacogdoches land-grabbing clique and the Galveston Bay and Land Company, made a flying trip to the United States to see the company president, Anthony Day, a New York banker close to President Jackson.

Steve wrote Williams that the Galveston land people had never forgiven him "for opposing their schemes to make a territory of Texas and their monopolies of land . . . etc. Tony [Butler] and they are birds of the same feather. . . . I have reason to believe that Mason and Mexía would keep me in a dungeon for years."

As early as June, Santa Anna had ordered Steve's release, but the corrupt Coahuila-Texas government, in the hands of land jobbers, had blocked this. The acting governor and the purged legislature were tossing out great, juicy chunks of Texas to the dogs of plunder. Among the recipients were Jim Bowie, gathering in vast areas, and Colonel Ben Milam, who had obtained his first concession as early as 1826. General John Mason, asking for a mere 20 million acres, raked in nearly half a million. Bowie was in on the deal as commissioner. Another land-grabber, José María Carbajal, was a secret agent of Samuel Swartout, whom Sam Houston also represented. Swartout boasted loudly and frequently that Houston would become "king of Texas."

Swartout, an intimate friend of Jackson, had been part of Aaron Burr's treasonable conspiracy but was now port collector of New York. He provided the great scandal of Jackson's administration by stealing over a million dollars. To "swartout" became the season's expression meaning to "swindle."

Though Steve's grants to relatives did not permit him to be overpious, he had opposed wholesale looting. The last thing the land-grabbers wanted was his release from prison. Nasty cliques in Mexico City and in Texas were determined to keep him behind bars.

2

The corrupt Coahuila-Texas government also insisted on Steve's continued detention because of Sterling Robertson, of Tennessee. Robertson was publishing scurrilous vilifications of Austin and using trumped-up evidence, plus bribes, to get hold of a defunct land grant north of Steve's colony on which to settle 800 families.

Robertson had an interest in a Nashville, Tennessee, company. In 1826 he and others explored the grant but did not settle. In 1827 Hosea H. League, bearing credentials from the Nashville company, asked Austin to help him get the transfer of the grant to the company made legal and to secure extensions of boundaries and the time limit for settlement.

Steve secured everything except the time extension. Had it not been for his efforts, the Tennessee people would have held only a worthless scrap of paper.

Sterling Robertson, representing the Tennessee company, came out in October, 1830, to settle nine families, apparently unaware that his entry was illegal on two counts. The law of April, 1830, forbade new settlements by Americans, and the company's grant had been suspended for failure to put settlers on it. The commander of the Mexican military post ordered the nine families, camped at the Brazos River crossing, to leave the country. Robertson pleaded ignorance of the law, the heavy expense incurred, plus the pressing need to put in crops. He wrote a personal plea to Political Chief Ramón Músquiz in San Antonio. He also asked Sam Williams to request Austin to take the families into his colony.

Other facts leaked out. The families had been halted at Nacogdoches but had sneaked out at night. Colonel Piedras angrily warned Austin not to protect them or give them land. Austin smoothed Piedras down, but General Mier y Terán and Músquiz ordered their arrest and immediate expulsion.

Robertson's assistant sneaked out of the country and blithely returned—this time at Harrisburg on Buffalo Bayou—with eight more families. He was in difficulties again. He and Robertson wrote desperately to Austin, then in Saltillo, to intercede for them with the Mexican officials. Steve asked Mier y Terán for leniency, and the general approved of the newcomers being admitted as settlers to the San Felipe colony.

Six months before this the Mexican government, determined to promote European rather than American settlement, had suggested to a wealthy French resident of Mexico City that he apply for the northern area which Robertson's company wanted. To block this, Sam Williams put in a counterapplication. Steve, however, recommended privately to Governor Viesca that Robertson be given the grant.

Governor Viesca grew furious. "You know very well," he told Austin, "that the law forbids that type of grant to foreigners. Robertson has flouted our authority. Technically he is a fugitive from justice. Had it not been for your interest in him, he would be in jail." The governor suggested that, if Steve, a Mexican citizen, would apply, the grant would be made immediately; otherwise he would have to give it to the French concessionaire.

"That would throw the whole upper country into a tan-

gle," said Steve. 'It would be ages before the tract is settled."

A joint Austin-Williams grant was approved early in
March, 1831.

Steve had great misgivings. Robertson and the Nashville company, ignorant of the fact that land could not be
held legally or indefinitely for speculation, would likely
raise a storm. He urged Sam "to keep all quiet" for the time
being. "I am operating on a pretty big scale for a taciturn
and noiseless man. The only object I have is the general
prosperity of us all and particularly the nation and government."

Steve soon deeded his share of the new grant to John
Austin, of Brazoria, in exchange for his personal note to
pay $6,000. Steve never received a cent of this but, after
John died of cholera, found himself liable for thousands of
dollars to his estate.

Steve was dreadfully upset when John Austin and Sam
Williams took Jim Bowie and others into the deal and began selling settlement rights—wildcat speculation for
which Steve knew he would be blamed. Repeatedly he
warned them to keep clear of land jobbing. "Such speculations are a curse to any country" and could be "a sore curse
to me personally." Not long after, Steve found himself in
prison in Mexico City.

Robertson plotted to get hold of the grant. He had
twisted documents drawn up in his lawyer's office and
authenticated, without witnesses, by a pliable judge.
Neither Williams nor Austin even got wind of this. Robertson also secured a false affidavit from the San Felipe
ayuntamiento that 100 families had been settled on the

Nashville grant prior to April 6, 1830; hence, the cancellation of the grant had been illegal. Actually not one family had been so settled.

Robertson's star witness was Steve's neighbor and shady foe, Buck Pettus. The dates given by him and Robertson were wholly false. Buck claimed that Austin had invented the yarn that Robertson had been ordered deported in order to pose as his benefactor. Pettus also accused Austin of having kept Hosea H. League in chains for sixteen months to hurt the Nashville enterprise and block settlement.

The charge against hotheaded League was murder. Steve, though no longer an official, had tried to help him obtain bail, but the Saltillo Supreme Court refused to release the prisoner. League's long detention had nothing to do with the land grant, for he no longer represented the Nashville company.

With his lawyer, Thomas Jefferson Chambers, whom Steve had helped secure the right to practice law in Mexico, Robertson journeyed to Monclova and got the Austin-Williams grant set aside. Austin wrote that he cared nothing about the Austin-Williams grant except to prove that his own conduct had been "correct." "I am in a distant prison unable . . . to repel calumny or defend myself. Chambers has so entangled the whole Upper Country that no man of common sense will settle there. It will do Texas great harm."

Not till January, 1835, was Sam able to set out in person with proofs to undo the mischief. He had the land commissioner suspended for improper acts. The governor, though a pro-Robertson man, admitted he had been grossly deceived. Robertson, who never had had any bona fide title even from the dubious Nashville company, was ejected.

During all this, Robertson and Chambers had worked to keep Steve locked up. Sam wrote, "Chambers bolted and barred your prison doors exulting in your sufferings. But it has ruined his political and moral existence in Texas."

Steve replied that Chambers's "boyish ambition and vanity" had caused him to try "to climb to the skies without a ladder." He looked at such a man as either Chambers or Robertson as "the captain of a noble ship does the worms . . . eating the sides of his vessel at a time when the waves are driving him upon a rocky shore. . . . The greater danger . . . absorbs the lesser."

20 · Texas Must Be Free

STEVE WAS NOT SO DESTITUTE of friends or support as he had imagined. Much had been done for him in Texas. Even his former enemy, the erratic Serbian, George Fisher, had sent the authorities letters and documents to help him.

When he learned of this, Steve thanked him warmly. "The only time to try friendship is when a man is in misfortune and persecuted by a host of powerful enemies. . . . You have interested yourself for me even at the risk of injuring yourself—I wish my family to know this—they will not forget it."

Thomas B. McKinney, the leading trader of Brazoria, wrote repeatedly to Steve in the strongest language, in the hope that his letters would fall into the hands of the authorities and be pondered. Blanco, Arizpe, Músquiz, Seguín, and others appealed directly to the government for his release.

Some colonists even discussed assaulting the Mexico City prison. At first they had feared to move lest they make things worse, but all the *ayuntamientos* sent memorials to the government and repeated them from time to time. The one that pleased Austin most was from Brazoria, signed by his enemy, *Regidor* William H. Wharton.

In July, Bell sent word to Perry that the new Columbia *ayuntamiento* was to be installed. "Better come up and let us make a trial of getting something on foot in Stephen's behalf. Peaches will be getting ripe."

The *ayuntamiento* advised the authorities that Austin's imprisonment was due to "false and malicious charges made by evil-minded and malignant persons resident in Texas."

The Matagorda *ayuntamiento* sent Peter W. Grayson and Spencer H. Jack, two able attorneys, to Mexico City to procure Steve's release. Settlers, including McKinney, Williams, and Bell, footed the cost.

The new political chief of Texas, Juan Seguín, son of Don Erasmo, helped the emissaries get a strong protest in Steve's behalf from the San Antonio *ayuntamiento*. Monclova, the provisional capital, was in great disorder due to a political coup, but the new governor affixed his signature to a strong petition.

On October 14 the two emissaries had a joyous reunion in Steve's cell and brought him the news that he had been overwhelmingly re-elected to the state legislature. It was a tremendous vindication. "No event of my life has afforded me more gratification," he told them.

Even so, the procedure was complicated and slow. "I

do not expect to get free before February," he wrote Perry despondently.

2

On Christmas morning Steve pushed back his earthenware plate of vile, greasy prison food. Keys clanked, and his cell door opened. The guard, smiling broadly, said, "Merry Christmas, Colonel Austin. You have been freed."

Thanks to Victor Blanco and the legal efforts of attorneys Grayson and Jack, Steve was released on bail provided by Bill Parrot, his agent. Don Victor was on hand to invite him to Christmas dinner.

After his ten months behind bars, the world glistened, the air was clean and crisp, the sun good. Just to see people freely walking about was a glorious sensation.

"Being allowed bail is almost full acquital," he wrote. He expected the affair to be wound up in a month, and he would be in Monclova when the legislature convened. He told Don Victor that his maltreatment would not deter him in his fight for statehood.

Nothing moved, but Steve pinned hopes on an amnesty law promised by Santa Anna for February and wrote Williams confidently that he would set out for Monclova by March 1. But by that date there was still no pardon.

Steve was not idle. He pushed proposals for Texas mail routes, shipping, communications, and road building. "If restless folk in the colonies will survey such routes instead of making trouble, they will be doing something useful," he said.

He published an *exposición* about Texas that had great influence. It was soon reinforced by the public report on Texas by Santa Anna's investigator, attesting to the extraordinary progress of the region. It denounced land-grabbing, cited other abuses, and advocated far-reaching reforms.

Steve made up for his long prison isolation by a round of entertainments. He mixed with leading intellectuals, went to the theater and the opera, and joined crowds watching a balloon ascension at Chapultepec. Offut, of the Washington Hotel, lent him a good horse, and daily rides helped to improve his health.

Not till March did an amnesty law go to the president. He sent it back to be modified. This would require still another month.

To Perry, Steve groaned that the trip had cost him $10,-000, a dead loss, besides imprisonment. He was grieved about Emily's having been laid up for two weeks with fever. "Tell her to keep up good spirits and laugh at all the slander of my enemies. Love to the children. Keep up the school."

Sam was downcast by the latest destruction of hopes for Steve's quick return.

God knows . . . how you bear up under the horrible reality of *mañana* and *pasada mañana*—a tantalizing procedure. With all the rhetoric and . . . feeling I possess I have urged the governor to send a fresh appeal, as a duty to a fellow citizen and to the citizens of the part of the state that cannot much longer bear with such a course in silence.

Sam reported that immigrants were flooding into Texas in droves, by hundreds, by thousands. Texas had suddenly fired the romantic imagination of the whole world. It was the newest El Dorado. Romantic tales floated to the United States, across the Atlantic to Europe, and to all parts of the earth. How would the development of this region affect the world's balance of power? Would it halt the advances of the "Colossus of the North" across the American continent?

Much of this new interest had been aroused by books and articles by Mary Holley. "Texas, Minerva like," she wrote, "suddenly came forth to challenge the admiration of the world."

Through Victor Blanco, Steve talked with Santa Anna again. The dictator suavely expressed the hope that Austin's imprisonment had not been too onerous and invited him to accompany him on a trip to Texas. Steve no longer trusted him or his harsh militarism.

April rolled into May. Perry wrote that they had thought he was already on his way back. "Such procrastinations and disappointment are truly vexatious. . . . What can be done for your speedy discharge? If money will answer any purpose, we will leave nothing undone."

Not till May 3 was an amnesty law finally published. Steve had to present an incredible number of documents to qualify. On July 11 he was granted a passport, seventeen months after he had fallen into the toils.

By then much of the country was in revolt. Santa Anna's troops had ruthlessly suppressed the elected state governments at Zacatecas and Monclova. Another violent incident had occurred at Anahuac, and the Texan question was growing ugly again. The government was threatening to swamp the region with troops; friends warned Steve that he might be rearrested and advised him to get out of Mexico City quickly.

He hurried by regular stage to Veracruz and there took a ship to New Orleans. He arrived there on August 1.

3

The langorous Creole city gave him a sensation of vast freedom. He loitered in the shops, buying things needed in Texas and presents for the Perrys and friends. On Charles Street he browsed in bookstores and purchased books. Among them were Sismondi's *Fall of the Roman Empire, Letters from Constantinople, Voyage of the Potomoc,* Scott's works, Irving's *Conquest of Granada,* Johnson's *Dictionary,* and McIntosh's *Revolution.*

To Mary Holley, who had moved to Lexington, Kentucky, he wrote that he would henceforth work for full independence. In spite of his dislike of slavery, he saw no other road for Texas than to become part of the United States. From now on nothing would abate his efforts to "Americanize Texas."

"All that is now waiting is a great immigration of good and efficient families this fall and winter . . . from Kentucky, Tennessee, everywhere, passports or no passports, anyhow," each man with his rifle or musket. "A gentle breeze shakes off the ripe peach," and by the end of winter, the "violent political convulsions of Mexico" would "shake off Texas" as soon as it was "ripe enough to fall."

And so Gómez Farías—that great but arbitrary reformer, vacillating yet brutal when in power—had done his country one of its greatest injuries by his unjust persecution of Austin. He had alienated one of the best American friends Mexico had ever had in Texas.

Not that Steve harbored personal animosity. He had greater talent than most men for overlooking personal injuries and never once spoke ill of the exiled president. What Gómez Farías had done was to smash Steve's faith in patient methods of reason and compromise and in Mexican leaders. Brought face to face with Mexican brutality and corruption, Steve no longer believed in the validity of Mexico's fine laws. Military tyranny was being riveted anew on the necks of the people in a way that no freedom-loving American could endure. And so, blundering Gómez Farías helped put iron into the soul of the greatest leader of Texas. His petty spleen helped lose an empire for his country.

21 · War

Trouble had flared again on the Brazos. Angered by criticisms and molestations of his soldiers carrying correspondence, the new Anahuac commander, Captain Antonio Tenorio, by-passed the civil authorities and arrested a Brazoria merchant and a friend for constantly sneering at Mexicans.

In June, 1834, before Steve was released, William Barret Travis, one of the Firebrands close to Wharton and Bowie —who had had a taste of the guardhouse under Bradburn —stormed Anahuac with twenty-five men and released all prisoners. His hotheaded conduct was roundly condemned, but the damage was done.

The government moved faster than ever to bring Texas, like the rest of Mexico, under the military boot. Even before Steve left Mexico City, Santa Anna, like Bustamante, overthrew the 1824 constitution which Texans considered the bulwark of their liberties. He abolished Congress and replaced all state governments with military rule. When Zacatecas held out for state rights and its own militia, Santa Anna punished it with blood and fire, massacring the residents, delivering the capital over to be looted and burned in an orgy of drunkenness, murder, and rape. Coahuila-Texas was next in line for maltreatment.

The situation in Monclova provided a perfect pretext. Governor José María Viesca, once more in office, had been authorized by the legislature to dispose of an additional 7 million acres in any way he saw fit—another vast spoliation of Texas. Sam Williams, Steve learned years later, was one of those who secured enormous grants on the promise of raising militia to guard the settlements against the Indians. He and other land-grabbers stirred up the settlers' fears of Mexico and Indians so as to stampede them into mobilizing with their arms in order to claim that they had fulfilled the contracts. This had delayed Steve's release.

General Martín Perfecto Cos, Commander of the Northern Provinces and a brother-in-law of Santa Anna, was ordered to move on Monclova to put an end to such plundering and to overthrow the elected government. This act would rivet militarism on the people, and the people were terrified because his forces were augmented by the "vandals" who had just looted Zacatecas.

The Monclova land jobbers fled to San Antonio and on to San Felipe. Only Ben Milam, who fought Cos's advance in the ranks of the local militia, was captured. He and Governor Viesca were roughly treated and lodged in prison in Monterrey.

James B. Miller, Alcalde of San Felipe, who had aided the

Robertson-Chambers land steals, issued a fiery proclamation calling for a march to rescue the governor and bring him to Texas to re-establish the state government.

A Firebrand meeting, spearheaded by the land-grabbers who feared that their grants would be canceled, adopted resolutions denouncing Santa Anna's violations of federal and state constitutions. It was decided to capture San Antonio, seize the military supplies there, and install Vice-Governor Ramón Músquiz as acting governor till Viesca was released.

Shortly before this, Lorenzo de Zavala broke with Santa Anna and fled to his San Jacinto estate in Texas. He warned Santa Anna bluntly that the liberalism and the justice he had trampled under foot would overthrow his tyranny. General Cos sent an ultimatum to the colony to hand him over. This was soon followed by a demand for other outspoken Texans: Travis (for his Anahuac assault), Sam Williams, Miller, Moseley Baker (another big land speculator), and others. Cos threatened to move all his cavalry into Texas and seize them.

Though more reasonable than Cos, Domingo de Ugartechea, now commander in San Antonio, still smarting from his earlier defeat at the hands of the embattled farmers of Brazoria, fired the difficulty with alarmist reports of agitation among the flood of Americans coming in since the lifting of the 1830 ban. There were now 10,000 in Austin's colony alone. He told of secession plots.

There was basis for his fears. Bowie, Wharton, the old Fredonian conspirators, former filibusters, and others were pulling in and out of Nacogdoches to confer with Houston, whose plans went deep.

Now Cos had sent an ultimatum backed by veteran troops ready to march.

2

The colony split violently between a war party and a peace party. The peace party had hotly condemned Travis's attack on Anahuac and roundly denounced the resolutions to march on San Antonio and Monclova. All the trouble, it claimed, was due to a few Firebrands, smugglers, and land speculators who had stampeded out of Monclova. Cos had done right in cleaning out the undesirables.

One settler wrote, "Our country is again assailed by aspirants and speculators, deceiving the people to sustain their Mammouth Speculation."

James Kerr, founder of the town of Gonzalez, wrote that Williams, Johnson, Bowie, and others cry, "Wolf! Wolf! . . . destruction, war, to arms!" Unless they fight, they won't get their titles. These "delinquents . . . against the laws of the country and . . . honor and morality" are involved in the illicit buying and selling of vast tracts in Monclova. War would be "disastrous for Texas, and would merely save some ten rascals" who had appropriated land.

Among those most decrying war was Austin's close friend, merchant prince McKinney, of Brazoria, who had worked constantly to get him released from prison. McKinney thought that the fight for independence was merely a ruse of power-hungry politicians wishing to load Texas with a great debt that it could not stand and get their hands on vast sums to squander.

Still hoping for a solution, the peace party sent emissaries to the Mexican authorities. Ugartechea strengthened the war group by refusing to let the peace delegates see Cos until all the persons demanded were delivered. Cos was said to be advancing on San Antonio by forced marches. Another report had him coming directly to East Texas by sea. He was said to be a hater of American-born Texans, believing that they had no rights and should be driven out, and doubly arrogant because of his close relationship to Santa Anna.

On August 7, 1835, Zavala published a manifesto boldly accusing Santa Anna of treason. The dissolution of all state legislatures had destroyed all popular obligation of obedience.

Bowie visited Columbia, and on August 20 a Committee of Fifteen there called for a new convention to meet on October 15. Travis, his ears singed by the angry peace party, feared they were moving too fast and wrote Bowie that they had better "be quiet and settle down for a while" until we are united. Bowie went on to Nacogdoches to talk with Sam Houston and then rode off on a private spying expedition on the Mexican side.

He barely eluded Cos's clutches in Matamoros and warned Alcalde Miller that vessels were being outfitted to take troops and supplies to Texas; 3,000 men had already reached Saltillo.

It was at this dark juncture that Austin returned, with the idea of winding up his affairs and settling quietly on a farm or traveling abroad, only to be tossed back into the fiery furnace of political affairs and threatened war.

3

The official reception that Austin received at Brazoria when he had come with Colonel Mexía was nothing compared to the spontaneous welcome he now received. People seized him by the hands; tears rolled down their cheeks. They came riding in like madmen from every corner as the exciting news of his return swept all Texas with joy and confidence.

He wanted most to see his family, the Perrys and the children, and rode off at once to Peach Point. He got there in the late afternoon of September 1, just before it started to rain.

He was sad to find Emily so frail and to learn that Mary had died, but the other children were healthy. Little Stephen, now nearly eight, was swift and gay. Perry, broadened in mind and spirit, was handling his affairs ably. While Steve was in trouble, he had been a pillar of strength for all the Austinites.

Early in the morning cousin Henry Austin rode in. Having heard of Steve's return the previous evening, he had saddled his horse and, not even stopping to eat, had ridden till dawn through swamps and driving rain. He was a sad, lonely man these days; his wife was dead and his children were in Lexington with Mary Holley. He wrote her that Steve's arrival had "united all parties." The Texans would now be "as safe as the Israelites in the land of the Philistines."

Cordial messages poured in on Steve from all the colony

and beyond, from individuals, officials, and *ayuntamientos*.

A big, official banquet-ball was arranged for September 8 to honor his homecoming. People waited breathlessly for the event. According to the stand Steve took there, the fate of Texas in this new dark hour of tyranny would be decided.

What would his position be now, when all Texans, even the mildest, felt that their homes, their liberties, their very lives were in danger from Santa Anna's bloody troops? Austin had always advocated conciliation and caution. Would he still maintain that stand? Would it be war or peace? The fate of Texas hung on his words at the Brazoria banquet.

He did not divulge his plans or ideas to anybody. Independence was now his goal. But when? How? The best moment? Was it too soon? Which course would be better? These questions raced through his mind as he carefully weighed all possibilities and prepared his speech.

4

The great feast was spread in Mrs. James Long's tavern. Mrs. Long was the widow of an early filibuster who had been executed. She and her children had been left starving in the wilderness among savages, but all survived and she acquired the title "Mother of Texas."

Sixty banquet covers were sold at seven dollars a head, but three times that number of men were present. Stephen was received with cheers. Henry Austin, though he complained that the dinner had cost him a new thirty-dollar suit he didn't need, wrote Mary Holley, "You never saw such enthusiasm."

As Austin rose to speak, he saw numbers of old friends who had shared with him the darkest days of early settlement, who had ridden with him to punish the Indians, who had been with him on surveying parties and in the councils of the government. Bell had come in from his Columbia ranch; McKinney, up from his warehouse on the lower river; Bill Dewees, from the Colorado. But many faces were absent: those who had given up and gone back; those killed by Indians or privations; John Austin, swept away by cholera. Most were new faces, part of the new tide flowing strongly across the frontiers.

Steve spoke simply, decisively. This was no place to tell of his troubles. All he wished to say on that score was that he had in no way compromised the rights of Texas. "Those rights belong to the people and can only be surrendered by them." He had hoped to find Texas at peace; instead it was "in commotion, all disorganized"—threatened with "immediate hostilities." This was not the fault of the people but was the inevitable consequence of revolution and "the imprudent and impolitic measures" of both the federal and state governments.

The government was seizing Texas shipping—"acts of piracy, committed under cover of the Mexican flag." Santa Anna had promised Texas special consideration, but he was sending an armed force. Only the people could decide whether they wished to submit and give up their rights under the 1824 constitution. "Let all personalities or divisions or excitements or passions or violence be banished from among us. Let the general consultation of the people of Texas be convened . . . speedily. Let it be composed of the best, the most calm and intelligent and firm men in the country. Let it decide what to say to the central government."

He did not mention independence, but he did speak of freemen speaking their minds freely and deciding their own fate. This was a call to calm reason, but at a moment of military dictatorship it was rebellion. It was a call to arms.

His ideas had traveled far since the glittering days of Iturbide's court. Openly endorsing the latest Firebrand consultation, he took the reins away from his personal enemies and won their support. He also obliged all reasonable and thoughtful citizens to join in. He became the leader of both parties on a democratic program. The best judgment of the best Texans would prevail by democratic decision.

He had merely stated his convictions without fanfare, but they met the needs and hopes of the hour. There was applause, and joy brightened every face. Men rushed up to shake his hand, to slap his shoulder.

Tables were quickly cleared away, music struck up, and some eighty couples "made the splinters fly" gaily till sunup. But right after his talk, Steve sprang to his horse and rode all night to San Felipe.

5

His house was dismantled, half fallen in, and a chimney was broken. He lived with Sam Williams until Perry could send up furnishings. Sam was leaving in a few days for the United States to try to raise capital for a Bank of Texas.

A preliminary San Felipe conference was held on Sep-

tember 12 at Johnson's tavern. Austin was made president,
and Patrick C. Jack, secretary. It was voted to support the
1824 constitution which President Santa Anna had suspended. A permanent Committee of Vigilance and Safety
was formed with Austin, Buck Pettus, Gail Borden, Jr.,
and others. The future milk king, Borden, was a former
San Felipe blacksmith who now owned and edited the
Texas Telegraph.

Events moved too rapidly for the calm democratic decision Steve had proposed. The enemy was at the gates.
Give up the persons demanded, Cos ordered again, or he
would march in. Texas, he declared, had to submit uncon-
ditionally to the orders of Santa Anna and his new constitution.

"We have no rights except what the government thinks
proper to grant us as a favor," said Steve. "War then is
inevitable . . . impossible to avoid. War and peace parties
are at an end. We have no remedy but to fight. A volunteer
corps must be ready for immediate operations."

Already J. W. Fannin, Jr., a new militant arrival of the
Wharton group, called on the residents on the lower Colorado and Lavaca rivers at Caña Creek and Bay Prairie to
rally with their arms to face General Cos, then landing
arms, supplies, and troops near La Bahía. Two more troop-
ships were due.

"We have determined," Fannin wrote, "to raise a sufficient force, weak in numbers but . . . resolved to be free
or die."

In La Bahía, when people did not produce the horses
and carts demanded, the mayor and *regidores* were
whipped in the street and the people were bayoneted into

carrying the supplies on their backs. It was a taste of what was coming.

Steve sent word throughout all East Texas. "The sword is drawn, and the scabbard must be put to one side until the military are driven out of Texas."

Weary after his pressing duties, Steve uncorked a bottle of whisky that had been sent over from Peyton's tavern at the doctor's orders. A mistake was made. The bottle contained corrosive sublimate, and he burned his mouth badly. One teaspoonful more would have ended his days.

The fight was coming to a head before the Firebrands could meet, and the San Felipe committee sent out a call for one member of each local Committee of Safety to come at once to San Felipe to form a governing council. "A government, perhaps a nation, will be mapped out," said Steve prophetically.

Zavala, Grayson, and others lived with Steve to help carry on the day-by-day duties. A thousand things had to be done. "Once more I am the pack horse," he told Perry. Once more his house became a beehive. "Everybody congregates here."

6

Ugartechea forced the whole conflict by demanding that Gonzalez on the Guadalupe, the settlement nearest San Antonio, deliver an old 6-pound cannon that had been given to the town for protection against the Indians.

The clumsy old weapon had been used by a filibuster in 1813. The spike had been driven out, leaving a big touchhole the size of a man's thumb, so that it could hardly roll a cannon ball across the square. But it made a lot of noise that scared Indians, and the Gonzalez people liked it. Besides they weren't taking any such orders just then. Instead of giving up the old relic, they buried it at night in a peach orchard.

Ugartechea sent 100 cavalrymen, with infantry to follow, to seize it. Gonzalez had only eighteen men with guns, but it decided to resist. All families were moved out of town. All boats were pulled to the east bank. At John Sowell's blacksmith shop, Noah Smithwick and others helped fan the hickory charcoal and pound out crude round shot and cut up trace chains to load the canon. Old files were mounted on the ends of river-bottom poles for lances. They were to prove more effective for prodding oxen than for battle.

The Gonzalez Committee of Safety appealed to San Felipe: "Send what force you can collect immediately to our assistance. Don't delay about provisions. We have plenty. . . . Time is most pressing . . . the occasion most urgent."

Messengers "sped the fiery cross" from the Lavaca to the Sabine. Couriers were flying along the bayous. In all Texas Committees of Safety were forming, volunteers were enrolling, guns were being cleaned and oiled, and supplies were being put on mules, oxcarts, and wagons.

There were only three parties just then in Texas, Smithwick remarked: Some were for independence, some for the constitution of 1824, and the rest for anything just so long as it was a row. But everybody in East Texas was of one mind about the Gonzalez cannon.

The Mexican forces appeared through the pecan groves on the west bank of the Guadalupe on the twenty-eighth. Ugartechea was thrown into a pet because there were no boats, and an orderly had to swim the river with his ultimatum.

The Gonzalez citizens stalled him for three days, then bluntly refused to deliver the cannon, and decided to attack him before he could receive help. The cannon was dug up, "brushed" and scoured out, and mounted on four oxcart wheels.

Bill Dewees arrived that evening and crossed with a force led by Colonel H. Moore at a ford 15 miles up. They camped in woods near the Mexicans.

In the morning, in a pea-soup fog, Moore talked with the Mexicans under a flag of truce. If Ugartechea would join with them in fighting for the 1824 constitution, he could keep his present rank. The Mexican refused, demanded the cannon, and spoke of treason and his duty to his uniform.

The lifting fog showed the Mexican cavalry ready to charge. A tall, bearded Texan waved a white cotton flag bearing a crude sketch of the old cannon under a lone star and the words "Come and get it." The Gonzalez cannon barked and barked again. The whole line opened fire.

The Mexicans never charged. After a few rounds their ranks broke, and they tore back toward San Antonio. For the most part they were impressed convicts with no stomach for fighting. Promised only three dollars for the expedition, they had been given scarcely enough corn to keep alive.

So began the "Texas war," October 2, 1835, two years to the day after Stephen had written his defiant letter to the San Antonio *ayuntamiento* demanding free government.

22 · On to San Antonio

More humiliated than ever, Ugartechea appealed to his "worthy friend" Austin. He cited the Anahuac attacks and other rebellious acts, the land-grabbers "kindling the torch of discord," the treasonable treachery at Gonzalez. He asked Austin to help calm the "enemies of order" and the "crimes and abominations" in that "interesting part of the Republic." Give up the cannon and all would be forgiven. Otherwise he would march with "every kind of arms . . . to prove that Mexicans can never permit themselves to be insulted."

The San Felipe Committee of Safety gave the answer. Colonel Ugartechea, it proclaimed, was on the march "to fasten down upon our necks the yoke . . . to rivet upon our hands the manacles of military servitude . . . till every spot of our rich and fertile country" becomes "one wide scene of devastation."

Let the constitution of 1824, which still raises its dying voice from beneath the feet of military usurpation—let the free and impartial in Mexico and in the whole civilized world give answer from the mouth of their rifles. . . . Fellow citizens of Gonzalez have been attacked—the war has commenced. . . . Texas must be freed from military despots.

Ugartechea made one last appeal to Gonzalez. If the Mexican prisoners taken October 2 were released and Austin would come to San Antonio to talk with Cos, he would delay his expedition.

But at eleven o'clock on the night of October 9, in La Bahía, now called Goliad, Captain G. N. Collinsworth and his volunteers bashed in the strong church doors to "wipe out the shame of public whippings and bayoneting." The officers and soldiers inside surrendered. The church was packed with the supplies and guns sent in from Mexico by Cos.

By then Austin was riding with his nephew Moses Austin Bryan, at the head of 100 more volunteers, hard and fast toward the Gonzalez front. The call for him to come had been urgent.

He had delegated his supreme executive powers on the General Council to R. R. Royall. Before leaving, he had had to quiet the fears of the coast people.

Bell feared that the women would be left exposed to a slave uprising, Indian attacks, and perhaps a sea-borne expedition. Mexican troops were reported coming by sea from Campeche, in southern Mexico.

Steve arranged for more cannons, guns, food, clothing, volunteers, and doctors to be sent to the front and placed heavy supply orders in New Orleans. Twenty thousand

New Orleans Grays were already drilling, preparing to swarm to the aid of Texas. Creoles were training their own volunteer outfit.

Steve wanted no part of the field campaign. His health was so bad that he could hardly sit in the saddle. Lacking military experience, he felt that others were better qualified. But he could not ignore the appeal for him to come in person, for serious quarrels and disorders had developed among the back-country recruits camped in the two diagonal plazas under the magnolia trees. Only Steve could iron out the trouble, which was serious.

2

He found that the various elected "captains" and "colonels," some commanding only a dozen or so men, were jealously wrangling. Each wished to be commander in chief. Some wished to wait for reinforcements. Others wished to storm San Antonio at once. Others wanted to go home; the quicker, the better.

Steve called the whole force together. "Retreat is now impossible," he told them. "We must go forward to victory or die the death of traitors." He himself was ill, but he would wear himself out rather than submit to Santa Anna's arbitrary rule.

Over his protests a council of war unanimously elected him general in chief. The most insistent voice was that of John Wharton. "He will unite Texas; and he is the only one who can bring our forces into harmony. He alone has enough standing abroad to bring us men and supplies from the United States."

The best harmonizer was action. Immediately Stephen gave the order to march on to San Antonio at daybreak. The "Volunteer Army of Texas"—less than 400 men—headed toward the high cannon-mounted walls of the largest, most heavily garrisoned city of Texas.

It was a ragtag crew in buckskin, sometimes new and soft and yellow, more often hard and black and greasy. Some wore broad Mexican sombreros; others, tall "bee-gums," or coonskin caps, long tails hanging behind. They carried bulky bed quilts or checkered counterpanes or store blankets or buffalo robes. Boots and shoes were almost unknown; chiefly moccasins were worn. Socks were unheard of. Some rode big American horses; others, Spanish ponies, half-wild mustangs, or plodding mules. Many walked. They were armed with old weapons: squirrel guns, muskets, shotguns, a few American Yagers, Kentucky long barrels, horse pistols, flintlocks, broadswords, butcher's knives, or tomahawks.

Almost anywhere in the lines, according to the momentary zeal of the prodders of eight long-horned steers pulling it, rode the old useless cannon. The wheels shrieked like the fiends of hell till men's nerves cracked and they cursed. The axles got hot and the wood smoked. There was no water to cool them. Tallow did no good. At Sandy Creek the precious cannon that had caused the "Texas war" was tossed aside in disgust. The steers went into the pot.

3

Mexican volunteers from Goliad marched to join them. Big Ben Milam, just escaped from a Monterrey prison, rode in at the head of a sizable group. He was a weird sight. He

had replaced his prison garb with clothes from the captured
Goliad church. His pants scarcely reached below his knees.
His sleeves were a full 6 inches too short.

Bowie, galloping hard from Nacogdoches with four or
five Louisiana friends, came yipping into camp, Bowie
style, on a fast, little, gray mare, two pistols at his belt, his
famous bowie knife in his broad sash, and waving his rifle.
Austin made him Volunteer Aide without rank.

Others, with or without fighting reputation, received
posts or commissions: James Fannin, Erasmo "Deaf" Smith,
Travis, the Wharton brothers, Briscoe, Dr. Grant, and Ed
Burleson, an old-school officer but an experienced Indian
fighter.

The little army camped at mud-hut Cíbola, while Fannin and Bowie led ninety-two men of the Harrisburg Volunteers and Brazos Guards nearer to the city. Bowie sent
back a request for fifty more men and advised Austin to
move the army north of the city so that its provisions could
be cut off.

The following day the Bowie and Fannin advance
guard made a sortie up the river as far as San José Mission.
Nearby was the fine mansion that Bowie had built for
Ursula—never occupied since her death.

Once more Bowie asked for fifty additional men and reported that he was using the last of his own money to buy
beef and corn. "You know the materials we have—they will
fight and fight desperately but must Eat."

Ill feeling was brewing between Fannin and Bowie, both
vain and ambitious. Fannin disgustedly suggested that his
own place be taken by Sam Houston or Colonel W. D. C.
Hall, who was a trained man.

Fannin, a man of mystery, had attended the United

States Military Academy under the name of "Walker." Like Bowie, he had been a slave runner and smuggler. He had come recently to Texas, with plenty of money to toss about in behalf of the Firebrand annexationist party. He was young, well-dressed, always a splurger, and signed dispatches "Liberty and Texas—our wives and sweethearts."

4

Though Bowie was impatient to push ahead, Austin's hands were tied. Besides ten thousand details of getting up reinforcements and supplies and carrying on correspondence, a real crisis had arisen, both in the army and in San Felipe, over the "Consultation."

Half the delegates were with the army, aching for action, glory, and command. Few wished to leave. If they did— as Austin urged—half the army threatened to quit fighting. Volunteers late-come to Texas were complaining bitterly that, while they faced bullets, all the choice land was being grabbed by those in the rear.

In San Felipe the convention had to be adjourned from day to day for lack of a quorum. Delegates, worried about their families, the danger of Indian attacks, or slave uprisings, threatened to return home. Others wanted to march to the front.

There was trouble from treacherous pro-Mexican elements. Royall warned that Judge John A. Williams, an "out-and-out murderer," had fifty-eight followers actively aiding the enemy and had a coast vessel for that purpose. He accused some residents of causing trouble by openly opposing the war. The Governing Council recommended im-

mediate arrest and punishment. Austin advised prudence.
The Brazos slaves did revolt. Ringleaders were hung and
a hundred others flogged almost to death. The Karankawa
and Comanches went on the warpath, stealing, driving off
cattle, and killing. Only Sam Houston's influence kept the
Cherokee quiet.

He had been at Washington-on-the-Brazos drilling volunteers. At San Felipe he found the delegates squabbling
badly. Some were for annexation; some, for independence;
some, for statehood; others, for conciliation and peace.
Many were for mere home defense. Others wanted to carry
the war on into Mexico immediately.

Till a quorum showed up, the wild talk was useless.
Therefore, Houston dashed off to the front to round up
enough delegates to get the meeting going. He rode into
Cíbola on a yellow stallion so small that his own long legs
almost scraped the ground.

"What's this about not letting the delegates go to the convention?" he roared at Austin.

Steve explained the situation and called in his top officers to talk things over. Houston said that they had to come
right out for independence and start a government.

"I'm for independence," Steve answered. "I am even for
annexation to the United States. But the time is not ripe
yet. That would unite all Mexico against us, and we would
face full-scale war. For now we must stand only for liberty
and the 1824 constitution. That way the Mexican Federalists may help us by fighting Santa Anna. We would have
Mexican allies, perhaps nationwide revolt. Before we can
declare for independence, we have to win a real battle.
Only a victory will bring aid from the United States. We
cannot afford to be overwhelmed before we get it."

Houston was only half convinced. Nobody fully agreed.

"I'll follow whatever the majority wants," Steve added. "But every move we make now has to help our fight, not hinder it. Anything that helps victory is good; everything that doesn't is bad."

They talked with all the delegates. The problem was to induce them to return to San Felipe and to persuade the army not to disband. About twenty agreed to return. All the men were then drawn up and addressed by Dr. Branch Archer, a pro-Wharton Firebrand, W. H. Jack, Houston, and Austin.

It was an ordeal for Steve. Scarcely able to sit on his horse, he faced the cold driving wind and mist to tell the men that it was as necessary to organize a government as to fight battles. Otherwise the army would get no food and supplies. He himself would remain at the front as long as ten men stuck by.

Fewer soldiers walked out than had been expected. Those who remained, pledged themselves to stand by until San Antonio was captured.

To stave off more desertions, Steve ordered an advance almost before the dust from the departing delegates had drifted away. To the council he sent word that he was pressing on as fast as his force permitted. "I have but four hundred effective men. General Cos has about 800 or 900, and is well fortified."

5

The Firebrand meeting got under way November 3, 1835. The Wharton group—electing Archer president—wished to come out point-blank for full independence without weighing the consequences. Zavala spoke sternly against it, and the man on whom the Firebrands counted most, the strongest personality present, Sam Houston, argued against his old friend William Wharton.

"Do you want immediate annihilation?" he demanded. "Don't declare for independence until a military victory has been won over Santa Anna."

Bill Wharton never fully forgave Sam Houston for "throwing" the convention.

Archer also went back on the Whartons. He laid before the delegates Austin's memorandum of what should be done: Uphold the constitution of 1824, declare Texas a state of the Mexican Federation, appoint a provisional governor, maintain in force all existing laws, pledge the faith of the state to raise money and arms, protect the lands and interests of the Indians (this was Houston's chief contribution), nullify all land-grabs since April, 1833, organize a regular army, and name a permanent commander in chief.

All proposals were adopted with little friction. Henry Smith, of Brazoria, whose head had been deeply grooved in the first Anahuac fight, was made governor.

6

At the San Antonio front Steve ordered Bowie and Fannin to reconnoiter at the missions above and then fall back to the main encampment. Among those who went forward were Bill Dewees, Noah Smithwick, and Steve's nephews Joel and Moses Bryan.

Scouts pushed ahead cautiously. Occasionally a dry twig snapped as loud as a pistol shot. They paused and held their breath but heard only the rattle of leaves and the howl of a distant coyote. About noon the scouters reached Concepción Mission. The whole advance force then moved up and camped in the pecan and oak groves on either side. Small contingents were posted on the 6-foot dirt bluffs of the looping river. Ahead a level vacant plain stretched nearly 2 miles to the city walls.

A big San Antonio gun, mounted on a church tower, spoke out with a dull boom, and a ball shrieked into the dirt just beyond the camp. Another and another came with "a hiss no language can describe," Bryan wrote home to his family.

The main army had moved up to Espada Mission. Steve set up his cot and office in one of the monk's cells. Ill though he was, he worked late and then went out into the air to survey his little force around the campfires. A boy from Lavaca was playing a harmonica. He wore a coon cap and had a big bowie knife in his belt. Beside him was his double-gourd canteen, Indian style.

With this crazy band Steve had to storm San Antonio's high walls and guns. He went back to his cot but couldn't sleep. He climbed to the roof where he greeted sentries and paced till dawn.

Here, long ago, he and his little band of explorers had banqueted with Martínez, Veramendi, Bastrop, and Seguín. All the wilderness through which he had struggled was now covered with farms and fields and towns. Two of his friends, Veramendi and Bastrop, were dead. Martínez had gone back to Spain. Elderly Don Erasmo, now a judge, was cooped up in San Antonio, maybe sweeping streets, maybe in jail, maybe killed already.

Steve was worried because Bowie and Fannin had not

come back according to instructions. He was worried about Moses and Joel. If they got hurt, Emily would place the blame on him.

As the dawn mist curled up from the prairie, he heard cannonading in the direction of Concepción. Racing down the spiral stairs, he kicked aside the campfires and set the troops in motion.

7

During the night a Mexican force of 300 cavalry and 100 infantry and 2 artillery pieces had pushed down the wooded river bottoms to Concepción and in the heavy dawn fog of October 27 attacked the advance patrol.

A sentry raced back through the fog, his powder horn shot off, yelling like mad. Another man keeled over when a bullet hit the bowie knife under his waistband, knocking the breath and courage out of him. For four hours, Bowie later reported with considerable exaggeration, "the discharge from the enemy was one continuous blaze of fire."

The Mexicans crossed the river and moved across the plain, firing as they came. The Texans got their horses down out of range and used the river bluff as a trench. When the fog lifted, the Texans saw that they were completely surrounded.

Big Bowie, reckless of his safety, made the rounds. "Keep under cover, boys, and reserve your fire; we haven't a man or bullet to lose."

The Mexicans opened up with a brass 6-pounder and a 4-pounder. Canister shot swept through the trees with a terrifying crash of branches. Bugles sounded the charge.

A tiny group of Fannin's men at the edge of the bluff bore the brunt. Bowie ordered them reinforced.

Noah Smithwick heard a groan and whirled around. Captain Richard Andrews was holding his ripped-open stomach.

"I'm a dead man, Noah, but don't let the boys know it. Tell them to fight bravely." Then he keeled over.

Noah tried to raise him. "Dick, are you hurt?"

"Yes, I'm killed; lay me down."

Noah put his knapsack under his head and ran to face the Mexican charge, coming in four to one.

Three times the Mexican soldiers were thrown back, but a constant hail of grapeshot swept through the pecan trees. Nuts rattled down. The men filled their pockets and cracked the nuts with their teeth as they took aim.

"Pick off the cannoneers!" yelled Bowie.

A lanky rifleman pulled back the heavy hammer of his flintlock. The gunner, approaching his cannon with a lighted pine torch, spun and fell. Noah and Moses turned the captured brass 6-pounder around against the enemy.

The Mexicans fled across the shallow water in disorder, throwing away muskets and canteens. The cavalry deserted the infantry to its fate, and Texans on the mission roof poured in volley after volley.

Sixteen dead were left on the ground. Bowie triumphantly reported 100 dead, "including many promising officers."

As the smoke cleared away, Moses Bryan sat under a tree to scribble a note to Emily, who was sick and worried. Among the Texans, he wrote, only Andrews was dead and only two men slightly wounded. "Plenty of bushes and trees saved lives." Joel wrote that he had had no chance to distinguish himself.

When Austin's men came up on the double-quick, smoke was still floating over the field. Steve felt that Bowie should have pursued the broken Mexican forces clear to the city walls. Bowie haughtily blamed Austin for not getting there sooner.

23 · New Front

ACCORDING TO AUSTIN'S SPIES, Cos in San Antonio was having his own troubles with disobedience, bad morale, desertions. Most inhabitants were hostile and were hiding out to avoid forced labor. Many of his troops were conscripted Indian peons or convicts. As a result half had to guard the other half. The San Antonio commander and his men had been put in prison for cowardice.

All streets had been barricaded with adobe bricks and loopholes. House roofs and all the plazas were heavily fortified with artillery commanding every angle. All ammunition had been stored in the cathedral behind a dirt-filled palisade of two wooden walls, 6 feet high and 6 feet apart. The enemy had plenty of corn but not much beef.

To attack the city, a strong base was needed close by. The southern approach was too open. Austin, therefore, risked moving the army through exposed country and camped at the stone mill in a dry gully beside the Alamo canal about a mile north from the walls, not far from the river and near what today is Fort Sam Houston, the biggest army post in the world. Travis's cavalry of 50 men rushed out to cut off 250 horses being driven south to Laredo.

On the west side a Bowie party raided to within 800 yards of the walls and dug in. Bowie demanded "a more equal division of forces." Steve advised him the two forces were not unequal. Travis was constantly out scouting. Prisoners had to be guarded. Many men were down with fever.

To hold the stone mill, only 600 yards from the city and under steady fire from a battery within 300 yards, was difficult. Bowie resigned in a huff.

Steve proposed that the city be stormed immediately. The rank and file were eager, but only one officer favored assault; in the Bowie-Fannin force, only two.

The two forces were united, and again Steve urged an immediate assault. Instead it was voted to leave a small detachment at the mill under Burleson and Fannin and retire to Concepción to await reinforcements and an 18-pound cannon being brought from East Texas. Actually it was hopelessly mired in the Brazos mud.

It was a depressing move in bitter cold weather, and the little army dwindled. Deserters said sarcastically, "I'm going after that old cannon."

2

Heavy reinforcements and supplies for Cos were moving north. Austin sent out friendly Mexican scouting parties and raiders and ordered Burleson to intercept several hundred men under Ugartechea bringing supplies from Laredo.

Burleson stopped in at Concepción to plead that the two forces be reunited at the old mill. Another vote! Once more Steve had to march his forces back to the north side.

Such pointless shifting about racked everybody's nerves. It mirrored indecision, fear, division, and intrigue. Every day Steve encountered more jealous scheming. Bowie was in a huff. Dr. James Grant, a Scot, who had cheated Steve out of $200 when the latter was stranded penniless in Mexico City, was trying to lure the army into following him on a wild dash into Mexico to plunder the rich northern cities. What he really wanted, said some, was to get back the valuable mines he owned below the Rio Grande.

Steve read a message from the head of the council. Royall hoped no man would "desert the Noble Enterprise so boldly and manfully begun." The frontier could not be left to the "ravages of a cowardly foe." Texas would be sacrificed. "As for comforts, you shall want for none. . . . Wagons are on the road with corn meal, shugar, coffee and Bacon Flour some arms, cannon and Ball, Blanketts, tent cloth, shoes, etc." Clothing would be provided free.

The proclamation was already ten days old, but the supplies were scarcely dribbling in. There were no medical supplies at all. The troops jeered. Grumbling sprang from every lip. Discipline was bad. Soldiers shot off their guns whenever they felt like it, wasting ammunition. They maltreated even friendly Mexicans and insulted their Mexican allies in camp. Thieving, gambling, disputes, and open fights were incessant.

Steve wrote Royall, "In the name of Almighty God send no more ardent spirits to this camp—if any is on the road turn it back or have the head knocked out."

The Ayish Volunteers, coming up from a lawless frontier region, got drunk in Gonzalez and looted every house and store, bashing in doors and windows and shoving women, children, aged, and sick into the streets. Gonzalez people protesting to Steve said that they much preferred savage Indians around in preference to the Ayish "cannibals," supposedly protecting Texan liberties and lives.

Bryan wrote of desertions every day, some on the pretext of going home for winter clothing. The "army would be all broke up." The men were "tired of waiting for the cannon." Only about 450 were left. Of these many were sick.

More than ever Steve wished to be relieved of command and wrote the consultation, as he had many times. "A man of robust health" would do better, someone else "more competent. . . . My worn-out constitution is not adapted to a military command, neither have I ever pretended to be a military man. . . . It is an office . . . I never sought and tried to avoid."

He was unaware that the convention had already named Sam Houston commander, with but one dissenting vote. Wharton, Archer, and Austin were appointed to go to the United States to secure volunteers, contributions, and a million-dollar loan.

Though so anxious to be relieved, Steve was upset.

Houston had repeatedly said that San Antonio could not be taken with the elements then existing in Texas and advocated withdrawal. It was against Steve's nature ever to leave any task unfinished. He feared that his departure might break up the whole force. If he left before San Antonio fell, his influence in Texan affairs would be greatly weakened.

Things in camp improved somewhat. New recruits arrived eager for action, and the New Orleans Grays, 100 strong, were coming up fast from Goliad under Ben Milam.

By November 18, 600 men were in camp and in fine fettle. Steve's hope for a quick victory rose, but again his officers voted against an immediate assault. On the twenty-first such a strong urge swept the camp in favor of action that Steve boldly ordered a daylight assault. But at the last minute not half the officers or men would follow him. After one more appeal he asked the army to pick an immediate provisional successor. Old Burleson was chosen.

On the twenty-fourth Steve mustered the troops to thank them for all they had done. He asked for their personal pledges to stay till San Antonio fell. Nearly 500 men stepped forward.

Not for Steve was there to be any military glory. He had never desired it. All his life he had argued that the builders and planners of life are greater than military heroes. But he left the army with a feeling of personal defeat.

3

In San Felipe, Steve made a report to the provisional government. Though San Antonio had not yet fallen, General Cos had been penned up and war had been kept out of

the colonies. He pleaded for generous maintenance of the
Volunteer Army.

Everybody in San Felipe was bickering bitterly. The
council and Governor Smith snarled at each other in language ever rougher. Duels were fought. The council members almost had a fist fight over whether the forces should
be armed with butcher's knives or tomahawks. Houston ordered both.

At the front Steve's departure released old jealousies.
Officers schemed to get command. Fannin, more bitterly
opposed than any to Austin's plea for an immediate assault,
now wrote Houston, saying the city could be taken easily
with only 250 men, and suggested he share Houston's command as joint brigadier general. He could fill that post
"better than any other officer." His touching modesty was
not rewarded, and he schemed with elements in the consultation behind Houston's back.

A friend gave his opinion. "Steve, you couldn't do anything at San Antonio with such a gang—no discipline, no
law, a bunch of wildcats clawing each other. Your biggest
error was appointing men on your staff who wanted to be
the big cheese and who would stop at nothing short of
your ruin. Why did Wharton resign? Travis? Bowie? Are
they or Fannin or Grant or Milam your friends?"

Steve chided him. "When I arrived last September, I set
an example by harmonizing with all my personal enemies
to save Texas."

"Was there any good faith in the men you attempted to
harmonize?"

"We all have to sink or swim together. Let anybody who
can do the job do it. The best luck to him."

He started straightening out his personal affairs, left in

a bad tangle by Williams, and put Bryan, who had returned with him, to making certified copies of all titles.

4

Things got so bad at San Antonio that the officers voted
to abandon the siege and disperse the forces. Disregarding
the decision, on December 4 Ben Milam led 300 volunteers
in a surprise predawn attack. They broke through to the
main plaza and seized two stone houses.

Commander Burleson and Bowie, both opposed to the
move, remained sullenly in the old mill, giving little aid.
For two days the small valiant band fought desperately in
the streets. Milam was shot through the head while trying
to batter through the heavy doors of the Veramendi house.
Colonel Francis Johnson took over and hammered through
to victory.

Commander Burleson and Bowie then rode in to accept
Cos's unconditional surrender. The Mexican general and
his men were allowed to march out with their arms on the
promise never to fight again.

Bowie jumped on his little gray mare and raced across
Texas. He burst in on the San Felipe Council like a mad-
man, demanding a commission for himself. Not waiting for
a reply from the startled lawmakers, he headed for Peyton's
tavern. That same afternoon he galloped madly back to San
Antonio.

At the news of San Antonio's fall, San Felipe and all East
Texas went wild with joy. Steve was delighted. The victory
would make his efforts to raise money in the United States
easier. But he knew it was only the beginning of bloodshed,

not the finish. Most Texans believed that Santa Anna was raising an army of 10,000 men and that all Texas would be hammered by blood and fire. As Steve looked over all he had helped build, the blossoming orchards, the green fields, the snug happy homes, his heart was sick.

He rode down to Peach Point on his way to embark for New Orleans. He had a bad chest cold and a severe cough, and the weather was vile. Moses Bryan wrote home that he feared the cold north would kill his uncle.

Steve told Emily that Joel was well and that Moses had conducted himself bravely. He adopted little Stephen legally and gave detailed instructions regarding his property, arranging for generous gifts to friends if he should die.

Steve saw Henry Austin briefly and rode on to McKinney's to embark. Since the boat was delayed, he had Christmas dinner there.

5

Steve still believed an open declaration of independence was premature and urged the council to continue to support the 1824 constitution and the Mexican Federalists. They should provide Colonel Mexía with men, arms, and money to raise revolt in Tamaulipas. If he succeeded, Texas would be saved without fighting.

"They call me a Mexican, these days," he told McKinney bitterly, "because I wish to save Texas from war, because I wish to join with liberal elements in Mexico, and especially because I have been nice to Governor Viesca [who had escaped from prison to the colony] and to Colonel

Mexía who can be most useful to Texas. Why should such good friends of our cause be openly insulted? Our rough boys maltreating the Mexicans are going to do something that will bring no credit, only shame, to Texas."

McKinney, though he was outfitting two boats at his own expense for the Texan cause, was even stronger against independence. "Unless we stand up against the self-dubbed patriots, Texas will go to the devil."

McKinney suggested that Steve lay out a town at this point at the mouth of the river.

"I laid out San Felipe," said Steve, "and I helped start Brazoria, Columbia, nearly all the places, but I never made a penny out of it—all for dear Texas. I'm tired of it."

"Others made plenty. This will be right on your own land."

"It's a beautiful spot, a logical spot. I'll pass the idea along to Perry. He and you can go ahead if you wish— maybe he ought to make out a handsome map—you know how it's done—and sell lots. It would help me pay you and Williams and Bell for what you laid out to send Grayson and Jack down to Mexico."

Steve boarded the *William Robbins,* bound for New Orleans, along with the two Whartons and Dr. Archer. In his suitcases were a million dollars' worth of Texas bonds printed in the *Telegraph* office by Gail Borden. Steve was not happy about his commission or his fellow commissioners.

While he had been in prison, Bill Wharton had publicly threatened to shoot him. Doc Archer had become "a rabid fanatic," shouting for an immediate march on Mexico City.

Here I am, [Steve wrote Royall] going to save Texas with a Wild man and another I cannot act with, a man destitute of political honesty . . . more devoted to injure me than serve the country—men resorting to low intrigues for their own aims and . . . personal aggrandisement. . . . Associated with such men, what have I to expect? Or what has the country to hope?

24 · Texas to the Torch

THE DAY BEN MILAM stormed into the San Antonio plaza
Santa Anna—"the Napoleon of the West"—reached San
Luis Potosí, the main army supply center. He hurried on to
Saltillo to organize the invasion.

The Mexican leader was cruel and vain, cunning and
vacillating, but he was a superb showman, clever at using
pomp and grandiloquence or humble modesty and soft
persuasion. A dashing commander with years of rough-and-
tumble experience, he was able to strike with lightning pre-
cision with large forces. However badly he treated his
soldiers, he was their idol, and his love of cockfights and
such humble vices endeared him to the masses.

The Texan revolt had been brought on in good part by
his abuses, but now he called for a national "crusade"
against the "foreigner." For the Texan campaign he created
a special Legion of Honor—a star insignia with five ra-

diants, bearing the national arms and the motto "Honor, Valor, and Country."

He boasted that not only would he sweep all Americans out of Texas but, if the United States aided them, he would plant the Mexican flag on Washington's capitol dome.

All Mexico rallied to his call. The liberals and Federalists, whom he had betrayed, preferred to battle the Texans and crush freedom beyond the Rio Grande rather than to fight for their own liberty against the dictator. Austin's hope of deflecting Santa Anna's blow from Texas by aiding freedom lovers in Mexico turned into a pipe dream. Santa Anna united the nation behind him in a holy war.

In Saltillo he quickly assembled an expeditionary army of 8,000 men. Those Texans who believed the fall of San Antonio had ended all trouble were merely hiding their heads in the sand. They and the peace party—"the Submission Men" and the "Tories"—again very vocal, closed their ears to all reports about the military horde at their doors.

Equally foolish were the new Texan heroes, greedy for glory and plunder, contemptuous of the Mexicans, who wished to carry the war below the Rio Grande to Matamoros —and even to Mexico City itself—with only a few poorly armed, untrained men.

Though San Antonio's fall brought great joy, it produced no harmony. The picture was not pretty. The civil authorities wrangled constantly and forgot to send ammunition and food to the little San Antonio force. They forgot to write a single letter to their commissioners in the United States, who were raising money and sending in supplies. Bitterly the council members quarreled over every penny, every act, every policy among themselves and with Governor Smith. Appointments became a snarling dog-bone business. When the council members used a $500 donation from Tennessee for the army to pay themselves, Smith told them off in scorching tones. The council declared that his conduct and language, "repulsive to every moral feeling of an honorable man," proved "his early associations and habits to have been vulgar and depraved." He was "a disorganizer and a tyrant." They had been "miserably deceived" in him.

Fission went down through the army. Too many heroes lusted for command and glory. One army and political faction felt that San Antonio should be made the whole pivot of defense. Others wished to invade Mexico at once. Some wished to fall back and wait.

2

The only leader who saw the whole picture clearly was Commander in Chief Sam Houston. He got little cooperation, for he also had to battle against intrigue inside and outside the council. That body sidetracked him by ordering him to remain in isolated Washington-on-the-Brazos, a raw stump town of fresh shacks. He could not have gone near San Antonio even had he been so inclined. San Antonio victors grumbled at being commanded by a distant general who had seen no action and who had said their victory was impossible.

Foreseeing the bitter trials ahead, Houston wanted no part of the San Antonio front and was even more opposed to adventurous expeditions into Mexico. He was bending every energy to building up a disciplined force to face the big army soon to fall upon Texas with shattering fury.

All too soon he was faced with disobedience and disintegration among the fighters. Dr. Grant, wounded in the San Antonio assault, persuaded Colonel Francis W. Johnson (who had replaced Burleson in command) that they should march south to Mexico—where his mines were. First they should attack Matamoros. Ignoring all instructions, they left only a tiny garrison in the Alamo, mostly the sick and the wounded. Grant's final perfidy was to take with him all medical supplies.

Houston needed some veteran forces to delay the main Mexican army while he prepared. The ragtag runaways bound for fool's glitter and the lion's trap would leave all Texas open to attack. They themselves would be cut up and destroyed. He saw that he would never have a disciplined fighting force if he did not impose strict regulations. All would be lost.

In this he was backed only by the voice of Governor Smith, who was now hated by the council. A wave of enthusiasm swept the council and Texas for the foolhardy daring of Grant and Johnson. For the moment Houston had to pretend to go along with the idea of a Matamoros expedition, but he laid plans to circumvent both Grant and Johnson.

He made Fannin Inspector General and ordered him to Refugio Mission, near Goliad, to take charge of fresh volunteers coming from the United States. He ordered his good friend Bowie to march posthaste to the same point. Confident that he would have enough loyal troops to enforce his will, Houston dashed across Texas and overtook Grant at Goliad.

The Scot had already rifled the town of all horses and provisions. Fannin, on whom Houston had counted most, now had posted his own proclamation, promising his volunteers "the first spoils taken from the enemy at Matamoros." It was to be a race to see which disobedient officer could get there first.

Bowie had his own peculiar ideas and also disobeyed orders. He did not come at all and wrote that the salvation of Texas depended on holding San Antonio. "We will rather die in these ditches than give up."

The ditches for the death stand were almost abandoned. Colonel J. S. Neill, left in charge at the Alamo, sent word that desertions continued daily. He had only 80 effective men and no horses for scouting. Yet Santa Anna's advance guard, 3,000 men, was already at the Rio Grande. Five thousand more were ready to march up from Saltillo.

The news was staggering. Even Houston had never dreamed that Santa Anna could whip together such a force so quickly or that he would be able to march north till spring. Unless San Antonio could be quickly aided with more trained men and supplies than existed in Texas, it would be merely a deathtrap ringed by steel and fire. This made Grant's "piracy" even more idiotic. Matamoros would be outflanked, cut off, and the invaders smothered.

Houston grimly kept his own council and rode on with Grant to Refugio. There, next morning, a sweat-lathered courier rode in with the news that Houston had been de-

posed as commander in chief. Fannin's backstage intrigues
had finally borne fruit. He was named the new head of the
Texas army.

Houston spoke his sarcastic piece and rode off with his
aide through the night, his thoughts bitter. At one moment
he swore that he would trample down all opposition. The
next he wanted to throw up the whole Texan adventure
and "commune alone deep in Nature's solitude with the
Cherokee Great Spirit."

He took a furlough and vanished, some said to the wigwam of a Cherokee chief.

3

Everything went from bad to worse. In San Felipe land-
speculator Moseley Baker raised a mob to throw out the
government. Presently Smith, faithful to Houston through
thick and thin in his efforts to unite the Texans into a strong
force, was deposed. Lieutenant Governor James W. Robinson, of Nacogdoches, took over. Every day, divided councils, cowardice, selfishness, braggadocio, ambition, and
vanity brought misfortune and disaster closer.

Every day Santa Anna's powerful forces moved relentlessly north upon the Alamo. It was a lightning stroke—a
terrible, driving march across the northern desert, with men
dying of thirst and fatigue, dying of cold and hunger, dying
of bullets in the brain if they straggled. Some nights the
troops slept in nearly 2 feet of snow. Provision wagons and
men were sometimes swept off improvised balsa bridges
into flooded rivers. But Santa Anna rolled steadily north.

He left a littered trail of unburied bodies in his wake, but he descended like an avalanche upon the broken walls of the Alamo and its defenders.

By then there were about 150 last-ditchers, commanded by Barret Davis. Among newcomers was famous Dave Crockett, heroic Indian fighter. Thirty men had ridden in from the Colorado. But even then, facing disaster, Jim Bowie and Travis quarreled bitterly.

Travis wrote the governor that, though his post had been confirmed by army vote, Bowie had seized command. He had insulted Mexicans, taken private property, freed military and civil criminals, and when old Judge Erasmo Seguín defied him, led his men drunk into the public plaza shooting off guns.

Only a few days before Santa Anna's artillery boomed, did the two Texas leaders patch up differences and frantically try to strengthen their Alamo defenses and secure supplies for a siege.

Now Santa Anna was inside the city itself. He ran up the black cutthroat flag of no quarter on the cathedral immediately.

4

A fast courier sped into Washington-on-the-Brazos, where a new Texan convention was gathered, with a letter from Davis. His force had been under steady artillery bombardment for twenty-four hours. He appealed for help "to the People of Texas and all Americans in the World."

The governor of Texas sent out a call to "save San Antonio or in fifteen days the heart of Texas will be the seat of war." It was too late! Before his words even reached most settlements, the Alamo had passed into history.

Houston set out, but the story was already ended. Fannin could not get there because the whole countryside was swarming with Mexican troops and he himself was trapped. No other Texans could get there, only a few Mexicans. At the last moment thirty-two men under Colonel José María González—who had stuck by the Texans despite all the insults—managed to wriggle into the deathtrap and fight bravely on to the bloody finale. Cooped in the place were Susanna Dickerson, wife of the artillery commander, and her baby girl Angelina, a few Mexican women, and the Negro body servants of Travis and Bowie.

Santa Anna's artillery pounded away—more than twenty-four guns. The temperature dropped almost to freezing, and the defenders' fingers fumbled clumsily at the breech locks.

Bowie, taken deathly sick, tossed and moaned on his cot with fever, only dimly conscious of the cannonading.

March 5, 1836, when more than 5,000 men were in the city and the prairie about, Santa Anna penned orders for a four-column, predawn attack. "The first column will carry 10 ladders, 2 crowbars, 2 axes; the second, 10 ladders; the third, 6 ladders; and the fourth, 2 ladders."

The cavalry was to scour all sides to prevent a single soul from escaping.

At 3 A.M. Santa Anna took up a position 500 yards from the Alamo walls. Precisely at 4 A.M., just as the moon rose above the prairie, the bugles sounded the fearful old Spanish *degüello*, "the beheading"—no quarter, fight to the death.

The Mexicans swarmed over the walls like ants. They swept in to hand-to-hand fighting, using gun butt, bayonet, and knife, hands reaching for throats. Men were slaughtered at their cannons. The defenders were driven step by step into the inner rooms. Bowie, racked with fever on his cot, slashed out with his bowie knife, the weapon that had served him so long and so well, that had made him famous in the annals of the West, till he was shot and knifed and bayoneted into eternal quiet. Crockett died at his post. Travis fell sprawling against a gun carriage, a bullet through his head.

5

While men were dying at the Alamo, the three commissioners in New Orleans, Austin, Wharton, and Archer, were forgotten. While men were dying at the Alamo, independent Texas was formed in Washington-on-the-Brazos.

Why this remote primitive spot was chosen for a new convention is hard to understand. It was only a zigzag cart track through the forest with a dozen scattered shanties. The delegates had to sleep under the trees, and a norther of wind and rain swept the thermometer down to 33 degrees.

Word came from Austin that, to get money, he had had to pledge his word that the Washington-on-the-Brazos consultation would come out for independence. This was a complete shift in the views he held before he set sail.

All night, March 2, in a fireless shed, the paneless windows covered with cotton cloth to keep out some of the icy wind, the delegates worked to draft a stirring declaration of independence. Mostly it was shaped by Lorenzo de Zavala, the most educated man present, who knew of more abuses by Santa Anna than had been practiced yet on Texans. All the grievances were there: dictatorship, lack of civil liberties, militarism, lack of religious toleration.

Sam Houston was present—back from his Cherokee wigwam—as a delegate from Refugio, a place now in Mexican hands. The consultation made him commander in chief again.

March 6, a fast courier, plying leather and spur, dashed in with another Travis letter—the last he ever penned: "The spirits of my men are still high. . . . Hasten reinforcements."

One delegate moved that the convention adjourn, arm, and march in a body to the front.

"Madness!" retorted Sam Houston. "That is the army's job, my job. Here a government has to be formed." He rode off alone to the Gonzalez front.

At that very moment Travis's body, along with those of Bowie and Crockett and González and the 179 other dead defenders, American and Mexican, had already been thrown on the huge funeral pyre that was to burn on for two days and nights.

Houston received haughty warning from the "Napoleon of the West" that all other resisters would get the same "gentle" treatment. Stampeding deserters brought word to Washington-on-the-Brazos that the Alamo had fallen and that Santa Anna was already marching across Texas.

Some of the delegates fled on with the crazed deserters. Others got drunk. The chairman proposed that they adjourn to Nacogdoches, a safer place. But a bearded delegate stood on a bench and shouted above the panic to get on with the work.

By ten that night, March 17, a constitution was slap-sticked together. At midnight David G. Burnet, the land lawyer with the twisted face, was named president; Lorenzo de Zavala, vice-president.

Burnet, once a countinghouse clerk, had joined an early expedition to free Venezuela. Later he traveled alone among Indians all through the West. He was a pious man who did not drink or swear and always carried a Bible— and a pistol. In 1826 he secured a big Texas land concession, which he pooled with the Galveston Bay and Land Company. That company had certainly been a good school for Texas soldiers and statesmen. A Galveston Bay and Land man was now president. A Galveston Bay and Land man was vice-president. A Galveston Bay and Land attorney was head of the Texas army.

Noah Smithwick, San Felipe's early gunsmith, saw much of Burnet. "A man of medium size, of no particular type of features, there was nothing in his general appearance to attract attention, unless it was a noticeable twist in his face."

That grim, cold night in the Washington shed, he delivered "a pertinent address of some length," as he later described it, and moved quickly to form a cabinet. The new government was sworn in at 4 A.M.

After breakfast, when they met again—still gray dawn —a deserter dashed in, saying that Santa Anna's cavalry had crossed the Colorado. The deserter fled on.

The convention secretary stuffed the new constitution in his pocket and fled, never stopping till he got to Nashville, Tennessee. The sacred original document of the new, free sovereign Texas never was recovered.

The entire government fled in panic toward Harrisburg on Buffalo Bayou—70 miles through driving rain and mud. Mrs. William Robinson, wife of the late acting governor, had to go on foot because, in the rush to escape, someone had stolen her horse. Zavala had only a mule. By his side rode Jonathan Ikin, an English capitalist supposed to be ready to give the new free Texas 5 million dollars.

Singly and collectively, the government dried off before the fire in the home of Mrs. John Richardson Harris, widow of the settler who had founded the town in 1823. The Secretary of War, Secretary of Navy, and Attorney General slept on the floor before the fire.

6

At Gonzalez, General Houston found troublemaker Moseley Baker with 374 men, 2 days' rations, and 2 cannons. Houston rounded up 125 stragglers. Deaf Smith came in with pretty Mrs. Dickerson and her baby and Bowie's slave, who had been spared at the Alamo slaughter. That day thirty women in Gonzalez knew for sure that they were widows. News came that Johnson's force had been wiped out at San Patricio on February 27, though he himself escaped.

Houston put Gonzalez to the torch and started his bitter retreat. Deaf Smith was given the heartbreaking task of bringing on the women, children, aged, and sick. One blind woman, her husband just killed, wandered along with six small children. One girl walked across the Texas wilds carrying two heavy pails of water to put on the screeching wooden wheels of her oxcart so that they wouldn't burn up. The great Texas exodus, the "Runaway Scrape," had begun.

Noah Smithwick, riding rear guard east from Bastrop, saw a desolated country.

Houses were standing open, the beds unmade, the breakfast things still on the tables, pans of milk moulding in the dairies. There were cribs full of corn, smoke houses full of bacon, yards full of chickens that ran after us for food, nests of eggs in every fence corner, young corn and garden truck rejoicing in the rain, cattle cropping the luxuriant grass, hogs, fat and lazy, wallowing in the mud—all abandoned. Forlorn dogs roamed around the deserted homes, their doleful howls adding to the general sense of desolation. Hungry cats ran mewing to greet us, rubbing their sides against our legs in token of welcome.

All along the route Noah saw broken-down wagons and household goods scattered far and wide.

Part of the stampede was caused by groups of plunderers who rode up to farmhouses, shouting that the Mexicans were right behind. When people fled, often half-clad and without food, the malefactors looted their homes at leisure. Many such refugees perished from hunger or savage attacks. Ghouls and Indians robbed their bodies. One young woman reeled into a rear-guard camp on the Colorado, her clothes in shreds about her torn, bleeding body. She had just escaped from a band of Comanches who had bashed in the brains of her baby. Her other tiny child was still in their hands.

The first night of the "great retreat," Houston's forces reached Lavaca River. Then the Navidad. Then the Sandy.

Their food gave out, and they lived on prickly nopals and berries. Ten whole days merely to reach the Colorado! Frantic deserters, women, children, slaves, many sick, many without food, milled about the bank in terror, unable to cross.

News of catastrophes mounted. Grant's troops had been wiped out at Agua Dulce on March 7. Every man had been slaughtered.

By forced marches Mexican troops reached the river just as the refugees and volunteers got across. Again, retreat.

Moseley Baker wanted to fight. He always wanted to fight. He harangued the men, threatening openly to depose Houston. The terrified government also demanded that Houston fight—message after message. "The enemy are laughing you to scorn. You must fight," wrote frightened Burnet from what he thought was safe Harrisburg.

Scheming to get rid of Houston, he sent spies into the little army, who reported that Houston was drinking heavily or that he was using opium. It is not likely that either story was true, but Burnet believed it his duty to God and country to see that no such godless man led the Texas army.

Not so godless! A short time before this, interested in a certain young lady's affections, Houston had solemnly embraced the Catholic faith.

Houston's dazed, bedraggled men finally camped near San Felipe on the Brazos in driving rain. Learning that all Colonel King's men had been massacred at Copano on March 16, Baker and Martin Wiley refused to retreat one step more, and when Houston gave the order to march north through the night in the mud-drenched storm, many of his men left in disgust to join the two disobedient officers. Houston put the best face on it that he could by ordering the two officers to guard the Brazos River crossing.

Baker put San Felipe to the torch and crossed to the east bank. In the crackling flames of the first settlers' town in Texas, Peyton's tavern burned. Seth and Ira Ingram's store burned. Buck Pettus's tavern burned.

The gunshop that had once belonged to Smithwick went up in smoke. The stores of Dinsmore and White crackled in the blaze. Bob Matthews's tin shop melted away. The home and news shop of "Great Big Cotton" caught fire. So did Gail Borden's plant. The Whiteside Hotel, the largest building in town, sent sparks high into the night sky. Finally the big double log house where the *ayuntamiento* met, caught fire. Not the least of the losses was Steve's double-wing cabin on Palmito Creek—all that was left were two crumbling black chimneys. The desks that Perry had brought from New York and most of Steve's valuable papers, records, uniforms, swords, and souvenirs were wiped out.

With a handful of men Houston struggled north through the black ooze of the Brazos bottoms. They made only 18 miles in three days of torture. More men deserted. But others kept coming in, and when he finally camped beside the welcome lights of Jared Groce's big plantation house on March 31, he had 900 drenched weary recruits.

Here was good food and a loyal patriot. Groce, the first man ever to grow cotton in Texas—back in 1823—now had a great estate and 100 slaves. Here Houston had held his first early talks about future Texan independence.

Next morning the skies smiled. Hour after hour, day after

day, Houston relentlessly drilled his volunteers and gave them not a moment's rest, rain or shine. Two cannons and other supplies came in from the United States through Nacogdoches.

More bad news arrived. Fannin and his men had been captured. The recently arrived crack Georgia Volunteers had surrendered at Victoria, and in Goliad on Palm Sunday were put before a firing squad en masse. A cry of horror and terror went up from all Texas and beyond.

Mexican troops were now streaming across all Texas in a powerful three-pronged drive, burning, killing, and looking for Texans to fight, but finding few. The panic flight of thousands of women and children continued amid sickness and death, rain and mud, separation and grief.

Selecting crack troops, Santa Anna dashed for San Felipe. Behind him at a slower pace came Cos with reinforcements. Farther back came Filisola with 4,000 more troops.

At the Brazos ferry the "Napoleon's" swift advance was blocked for days by the orange-dotted firing of the long rifles of Baker's and Wiley's men. Suddenly Santa Anna gave up the attempt to cross and swung south at a fast pace. Crossing the Brazos lower down, he dashed for Harrisburg, hoping to capture the whole Texan government. The inhabitants barely had time to put their town to the torch and flee. Santa Anna raced on through to Ward's Point.

By a hairbreadth Burnet, his cabinet, and Gail Borden, editor of the *Telegraph*, escaped without food or supplies on a tiny wood-burning steamer to Galveston Island. There they were devoured by mosquitoes and had to sleep on the bare ground without blankets.

25 · San Jacinto

IN THIS DARK HOUR supplies and volunteers began pouring
into Texas from New Orleans for an army somewhere in
the Brazos swamps. News oozed through that Houston
would soon march south, and Burnet sent the Secretary of
Treasury on the *Laura* and the Secretary of Navy on the
Cayuga with volunteers and supplies shipped in by Austin and the other commissioners to try to contact Houston's
forces.

The three commissioners had been superhumanly active.
In less than three weeks after arriving in New Orleans,
they had arranged two loans totaling $250,000 at 8 per
cent, repayable in cash or in first-choice land at fifty cents
an acre. They were advanced $60,000 pending a declara-
tion of independence by Texas. William Bryan, a New Orleans merchant acting as financial and shipping agent,

provided another $100,000 credit. Donations and benefits were also collected.

By January 20, 1836, two weeks before the Alamo disaster, Austin and his two companions had bought three schooners and a 6-pound brass cannon. They turned over $4,000 to Houston's recruiting agent; $5,500 to Adjutant General John Wharton; $16,000 to the Quartermaster General. Before the month was out, supplies were moving out of New Orleans.

The Surgeon General bought hospital tents, blankets, medicines, surgical instruments, and other supplies. The Quartermaster bought 20,000 pounds of middling bacon, 15,500 pounds of coffee, 5,000 pounds of soap, 8,000 pounds of lead, 1,000 butcher's knives, 1,000 tomahawks, 3,000 pounds of chewing tobacco. He also secured saddles, blankets, sugar, beans, wine, whisky, vinegar, and carpenter's, gunsmith's, blacksmith's, and mechanic's tools.

Talks with Wharton and Archer had greatly modified Steve's opinions. The three men revised their estimates of each other and agreed perfectly on what had to be done. Thereafter they moved swiftly without the slightest friction. Steve wrote Perry that "the most perfect harmony" existed. "Archer is truly a noble fellow. . . . Wharton and myself are on the best of terms." He was sorry that they had not known each other personally before.

Steve had come around to their views on immediate independence, and he changed his attitude abruptly. They could get no money unless Texas became a sovereign nation. News from the interior of Mexico now showed clearly that there would be no revolt against Santa Anna. The Federalist party had declared openly against Texas and for Santa Anna. It was now definitely a national war in earnest.

To Henry Austin, Steve wrote, "The reasons for leaving open any door however small, for union with Mexico have ceased. . . . All parties are united against us. . . ." He wrote Houston that his long responsibility to the settlers had made him overcautious. Nothing could be gained now by delaying independence. The sooner the better.

Friend McKinney, shocked and hurt at Steve's somersault, wrote, "My confidence in you is I think forever at an end. I am not your enemy and trust never will be but . . . I am now fully convinced . . . you cannot be anything else but an injury to your country. . . ."

The commissioners went on to Nashville and Louisville. The whole Mississippi Valley was boiling with interest. Everywhere they found the greatest enthusiasm. "The hearts of the people are with us," Steve wrote Perry.

In Nashville icy weather laid the commissioners up with influenza and pleurisy, and Wharton had to remain behind. Steve went to Lexington to see his beloved cousin Mary. She was bending every effort to get Kentucky money and volunteers for Texas.

The three commissioners reached Washington by the end of March and put up at the National Hotel. Austin went on to New York. Archer toured Richmond and southern seaboard cities. Wharton strove to secure United States recognition from Congress and his friend and fellow Tennessean, President Jackson.

But a Mexican army of 8,000 was now ravaging Texas. The cold-blooded murder of Grant's men, the quarrels between Smith and the council, the Moseley Baker mob, the strange dismissal of Houston, the mad "Runaway Scrape" —all undermined the confidence of the moneylenders.

By then Perry, Emily, Joel who had come home sick, the children, and the slaves were fleeing from Peach Point. Perry had wished to send Emily and the children to New Orleans by sea, but all boats were jammed, and he had to take them overland. Bryan Moses had gone back into the army as Houston's aide, somewhere on the Brazos bottoms.

"God knows," Perry wrote Steve, "when or where we will all meet again."

On April 8 the Perry family reached Lynch's ferry above Harrisburg, where they waited fretfully for the wind to abate so that they could get their wagons, horses, and slaves across, for Santa Anna was already at the Brazos.

The news from Texas was dark, but Steve tried to arrange a $5,000,000 loan through Nicholas Biddle of the United States Bank in Philadelphia. He also appealed to Jackson to aid the Texans—at the mercy of the aroused bloodthirsty Comanches and of 7,000 men "fighting under the bloody flag of a Pirate"—with some of the $37,000,000 in the national treasury.

Biddle did not respond, and Jackson, baited by New Englanders who were shouting that Santa Anna was right in putting the Texas slaveholders and land-grabbers to the sword, could make no open move. "Were not the Texans the real invaders plundering Mexico's sacred sovereign soil?" demanded the New England abolitionists.

Early in April, Wharton joined Austin in room 47 at the American Hotel in New York. Their whole bill for one month—for food, lodging, laundry, liquors, cigars, and entertaining—totaled only $304.66. Later they were accused of squandering money in riotous living while good Texans died.

The commissioners finally secured a small loan of $100,-000 from eleven individuals, of which $17,000 was advanced. These benefactors were headed by the notorious Swartout, who was trying to clinch his own land steal. On the strength of this loan, he later tried to put across a truly colossal steal.

2

As Santa Anna dashed after the vanishing coattails of President Burnet, Houston started down the east bank of the Brazos, his force increased by temporary "deserters" from the United States Army just beyond the Sabine under General Edmund P. Gaines, who obligingly looked the other way.

Houston's force joined up again with the Baker-Wiley outfits. But at the Nacogdoches road junction "Fight-or-Die" Wiley ran out on the army, leading his 400 men on a stampede of refugees fleeing to the United States.

Despite mud and storm, Houston did 55 miles in two and a half days. He reached Buffalo Bayou to find Harrisburg in smoking ruins. Santa Anna was near Morgan's Point in New Washington.

Houston got his men across the bayou in boats, logs—anything that would float. He himself crossed on a tilted, torn-up cabin floor. At Vince's bridge, they kicked aside the traces of Santa Anna's campfires and moved swiftly on through the night.

The Mexican leader was in a triangle of river, bayou,

and swamp with only two exits: little Vince's bridge or Lynch's ferry across the San Jacinto. A race for the ferry began. Houston won. At two in the morning his tired soldiers dropped in their tracks beside the 8-foot magnolia trees along the bayous and in deep oak woods draped with Spanish moss. Houston posted his only big guns, "The Twin Sisters," to command the San Jacinto savannah of waist-high grass.

Early next morning Santa Anna's gray-clad cavalry and infantry skirmishers topped the rise in two columns. An artillery barrage opened. A ball glanced from Houston's bridle. A colonel fell with smashed hip. The Mexicans dropped into the grass and wriggled away. The following dawn Houston's soldiers fidgeted, for their commander did not stir. This was his first sleep of more than three hours in six weeks.

While Houston slept, General Cos marched unopposed into Santa Anna's camp with strong reinforcements. Filisola's whole army was coming up. Why did Houston delay? Tension mounted to the breaking point. Before Houston had shaved, the sun was high that dramatic day of April 21, 1836.

Deaf Smith rode quietly off to chop down Vince's bridge in the rear—the only approach and the only escape left for either Mexicans or Americans. Houston quietly mounted his white charger and rode up and down the assembled lines. "Victory is certain! Trust in God and fear not! Remember the Alamo!" He wheeled and led the charge. It was four in the afternoon.

Santa Anna, waiting confidently for Filisola, sure that the Texans, not he, were trapped, never dreamed that

Houston, with every advantage of position, would attack across open meadows against strong breastworks and a cannon. The Mexican general had also risen late. Believing that time was on his side, he bathed and shaved leisurely. He was now enjoying a siesta. Cos's men, worn out from forced marches, were also sleeping.

Houston's "Twin Sisters" smashed a hole in the breastworks. Running stooped in the long grass, the Texans drove forward. Orange flames spurted at point-blank range. Texans fell right and left. Close before the breastworks, Houston went down from a blast of grapeshot, his horse killed, his ankle smashed. He mounted another horse. The Texans swept right over the top into hand-to-hand fighting. Houston's drilling had not been in vain.

The Mexican camp, aroused so abruptly from afternoon slumber, was thrown into milling confusion. Before the full defense force could man the breastworks, the line there broke and sagged back toward Santa Anna's tents—gray-clad men running, turning and firing, and running again. The officer and brigade holding the Santa Anna cannon went down before Texan knives. A colonel, rallying another group, was picked off by a sharpshooter.

The whole defense broke to pieces. Remembering the Alamo, the Texans pursued the fleeing gray-clads relentlessly without pity, slashing them down, granting no quarter even when they knelt and pleaded for mercy, clubbing them, bayoneting them, knifing them. A whole Mexican cavalry company was rushed over a cliff in a tangle of death into the bayou. Others drowned in the deep San Jacinto swamp. About half Santa Anna's army was slaughtered, and many more victims would have reddened the long

San Jacinto grass had not General Almonte managed to march about 400 men off in good order and surrender them in a body.

Houston fainted. His boot was full of blood.

3

When Santa Anna was brought in as a prisoner, Houston was propped against a tree, his face white as a sheet. The "Napoleon of the West," one of the first to flee from the field, was clad, not in his uniform and medals, but in a faded blue shirt and red felt slippers which he had found in a deserted shack. He had been captured sitting on a stump, gloomily looking at what once had been Vince's bridge. The volunteers would have cut him to ribbons. But his life was saved, some said, because he gave Wharton the secret Masonic sign. Brought before Houston, he asked for opium and got it.

Moses Bryan and General Almonte acted as interpreters.

"General," remarked Santa Anna, "such a thing as assaulting breastworks without bayonets or swords was never known before. And why under the sun did you let Cos come into my camp with reinforcements?"

"So as not to have to take two bites out of one cherry," was Sam Houston's cheerful laconic response.

Santa Anna agreed to an armistice, which he signed the next day, and sent orders to Filisola to withdraw his troops to San Antonio. One battle and a stroke of the pen had ended all hostilities.

Houston, kicked out of the army only six weeks before, now by a single lucky battle had become the great hero of all Texas. Texas was half-ruined, houses vacant or burning and people fleeing through festering refugee camps of pestilence and death. It was a Texas of grief and despair that early spring of 1836 that had been saved by Sam Houston, now lying on a blanket with a boot full of blood.

Steve Austin, who had provided many of the supplies that had won this battle, was forgotten. The man who had founded Texas and labored and slaved and gone to prison for it—fifteen years of arduous sacrifice—was forgotten. Houston was the hero of the hour.

Burnet came over from Galveston Island on the wood-burning *Yellowstone* and picked up souvenirs from a battlefield. Already heaps of unburied Mexican bodies—more than 600 of them—and dead horses were sending up a stench for miles around. Already buzzards and coyotes were tearing at the putrid flesh. Cows would soon be munching their bones.

Amid this overpowering stench, soldiers shouted for Santa Anna's blood. Houston was trying to get him to sign a treaty recognizing Texan independence.

Walking the hairline between death and personal freedom while the smell of rotting flesh and the cries of vengeance drifted into this conference, sodden with heat and bitterness, Santa Anna bargained cannily. The president and the cabinet could stand no more and decided to take the prisoner to Galveston Island out of reach of the soldiers.

Gangrene had already set in on Houston's smashed foot. Surgeon General Ewing said that his life could be saved only if he were rushed to New Orleans for an operation. Burnet, filled with cold fury that Texas had been saved by a man whom he so deeply disliked, clutched his Bible to his breast and said there was no room on the *Yellowstone*.

But the captain refused to budge without Houston, and Secretary of War Thomas J. Rusk, an early fighter at San Antonio, and his brother carried the commander aboard in defiance of the president's orders. Ewing, also defying the president's orders, went along to care for him. In a towering rage Burnet dismissed Ewing from his cabinet.

At Galveston the government and the prisoner transferred to the *Independence* to set up offices in Velasco at the mouth of the Brazos. Even then the president refused to divert the *Yellowstone* from its duties, so that Houston could be taken to New Orleans.

Not until May 13, three weeks after his injury, was the liberator of Texas able to get private passage—on a dirty little trading schooner, the *Flora*. He tossed on the deck with fever and pain through seven days of storm. As the little vessel nudged the New Orleans wharf, the crowd surging down from the levee almost swamped it. Houston motioned aside all aid and lifted himself on his homemade crutches to greet his cheering admirers.

The great hero looked like a dirty pirate. His coat was in tatters. His stinking shirt was wrapped around his shattered rotting ankle. He lurched against a gunwale and fainted as he was carried off. The surgeons removed twenty-two pieces of bone.

They did not believe the hero would live or ever walk again.

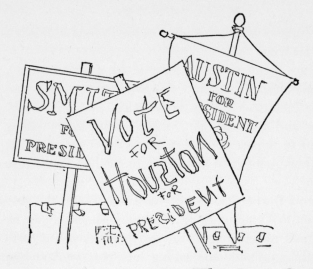

26 · The Last Campaign

"Santa Anna has been killed!" Such was the cry that greeted Stephen Austin as he stepped off the boat in Velasco, Texas, June 27, his head spinning from his usual seasickness.

The little town was in an uproar, people milling in the street and men in buckskins and coon caps racing along with pistols and guns. Soldiers were moving up on the dead run, an unofficered mob.

The two other commissioners had remained in Washington, vainly trying to get President Jackson to recognize Texas as an independent nation. By the time Steve got back to Velasco, Houston was on his way back, also, but collapsed in San Augustine, a little border town southeast of Nacogdoches. There he remained for many weeks, convalescing, his injured foot on a pillow. He was sweetly consoled by "beautiful" young Anna Barker, a romantic girl

234

who had come down from Nacogdoches to feed him broth and hold his hand.

The Texas army was now headed by dashing, young General Mirabeau B. Lamar, who had distinguished himself at San Jacinto as head of the cavalry.

Victory had resulted in a most unruly army. Some threatened to depose Burnet. Some wanted to kill Santa Anna. Others wanted to march off to further adventures in Mexico.

On June 1 Burnet had put Santa Anna aboard the ship to take him to Veracruz in accordance with the treaty he finally signed recognizing Texan independence. But fresh North Carolina Volunteers sailing into port yanked him ashore again. They riveted manacles attached to a heavy chain and a cannon ball to his wrists and ankles. He languished thus in the hot Velasco jail while the army and government were at bitter loggerheads. The mob wanted Santa Anna killed. So did the army.

But how could you kill a president with whom you had negotiated a treaty of independence and who was responsible for enforcing it?

"Remember the Alamo!" shouted the soldiers.

Burnet angrily blamed Houston for all his difficulties.

The day Steve returned a drunken soldier fired through the window into the little room where the president of Mexico sat staring at the heavy cannon ball. The soldier's aim was bad. Steve hurried to President Burnet and suggested that Santa Anna be moved up the river to Columbia out of reach of excitable, idle soldiers and the mob hanging around the new government. For the president of

Mexico to be killed by a savage mob would be an eternal blot on the new country's history.

Part of the feeling against the prisoner was being stirred up by General Lamar, the new army head, who was trying to promote his own popularity with the soldiers and the rabble. He was also promising new armed adventures in Mexico. Steve sent him a strong message that expeditions into Mexico would be pure folly and that no mistreatment of Santa Anna's person should be allowed. He also urged Burnet to stop giving offense to Houston and his followers.

"Any precipitate action by you," he told him bluntly, "at this time may create an excitement in the army and will do it." He sought in every way to calm passions, to bring the leaders together, to get the unruly army back under control and to head off new wildcat forays into Mexico.

When things came close to the breaking point, stubborn Burnet secretly rushed Santa Anna up the river to the country home of James A. Phelps, outside Columbia, where he was permitted to live free of chains.

2

Steve had come back to Texas with definite ideas to avert new disaster: to make the armistice stick, to bring about peace, then to make that peace permanent by gaining quick recognition of Texan independence from both Mexico and the United States. Only thus could Texas be saved from more devastation. He tried to put an end to existing anarchy by a positive program behind which all groups could rally.

So long as Santa Anna was a prisoner, he would be the big apple of discord. His person overshadowed all other personalities and issues. Hatred of him even threatened to overthrow the government. Steve had seen political mobs destroy civil authority and liberty in Mexico City and had not liked the ugly spectacle. He did not like such a threat hanging over the weak government of Texas. He tried to bring the people to their senses by stressing the dangers of another invasion and the necessity for preparing for it.

He wrote Lamar that General José Urréa, the new Mexican commander, was already marching north with 10,000 men and that 10,000 more were almost ready to march. If madcap adventurers set out, they would be slaughtered. It would be the story of Grant, Johnson, Fannin, and King all over again. Blood would again drench Texan soil. People's homes would be ravished. Every man must rally to the desperate struggle. He himself, as soon as he was able, he wrote Lamar, would be with the army as a private soldier.

The armistice had given temporary advantages. Otherwise it had been a foolish blunder, for no Mexican government would recognize an arrangement forced on a prisoner. After San Jacinto, Houston should have ordered his army to destroy all Mexican forces remaining on Texan soil. That golden chance had been lost. But fortunately, thanks to Sam, Steve added, Texas was now "far better prepared to fight. Texans have learned it is better to die in battle than to suffer a hundred deaths by exposure and fatigue."

But, though warning Texas of terrible new dangers, Steve sought to ward them off by peace maneuvers. Just as the armistice had been a mistake, so the independence treaty with Santa Anna had no validity. Forced upon a prisoner "in chains," it would be disregarded by his government and violated by him once he were free. Two things were now necessary: Get rid of the rotten apple of discord as quickly as possible and devise some scheme to make his treaty promise binding.

3

Steve hurried to Columbia and rode down the 2-mile avenue from the thriving little town, which had been miraculously spared the ravages of war, to Bell's handsome house.

Bell's good-looking wife was one of the most intelligent and gracious women Steve had ever met. Their two boys were now grown up, and one was in the army.

Bell was prospering. Not so many years back the Bells had lived in a primitive cabin amid a tiny field of corn. Those days the whole family wore buckskin. Steve recalled early visits when they had eaten at a rude clapboard table, using split cane stalks for spoons and forks, and had drunk out of little wild cymlings, scraped and scoured clean.

Now Bell had a handsome brick mansion, luxuriously furnished, a table with sparkling silver and cut glass served by Negro servants. Now the black walnut trees he had planted behind his house were gigantic. "Look at this crowfoot grass," said Bell. "It's marvelous. I keep a dozen horses fat on this one little patch."

Steve went over to the home of Dr. Phelps, at Orizombo, to talk with Santa Anna, who was being guarded by sullen coon-capped volunteers. Dr. Phelps had ushered one of Emily's babies into the world.

It was blistering hot, and Steve met Santa Anna alone under an arbor.

The general was nervous but not too dejected. "My friend," he began, "that you should come to see me here, a poor man in utter disgrace, is an honor."

"Once I was a prisoner of yours," Steve said sharply.

"That was one of my great blunders, my dear General."

"Your great blunder was that you didn't shoot me as you do with most prisoners."

Santa Anna's dark eyes flickered. "*C'est la guerre*," he said, shrugging. "Is that a suggestion as to what awaits me?"

"We have better use for you than that."

"Once, you recall," said Santa Anna, "you and I discussed Texas for three solid hours with my cabinet and good Victor Blanco, and, yes"—his face twisted—"with that black scoundrel, Lorenzo de Zavala."

"He is now vice-president of Texas," answered Steve stiffly. "When you persecuted him, you committed another blunder."

"Was I so unreasonable when we talked about Texas?"

"Nor am I here to be unreasonable. I come with a plan for your quick liberation. It depends wholly on yourself."

Santa Anna's eyes lit with fire, but his hands shook. Lack of opium had shaken him badly. To get it, he was willing to do almost anything. He grasped eagerly at this new straw and readily agreed to everything Steve proposed.

"I shall have to convince General Lamar. He does not like you very much."

4

At Steve's request General Lamar came over to Bell's house that night. He was younger than Austin, debonair, an art dilettante, and poet. He had been outraged at the government's failure to execute Santa Anna. When Steve said he had just seen the "monster," Lamar's face set coldly.

"I did not save Santa Anna," Steve reminded him. "The government did. Houston did. Santa Anna merited death. But it will always redound to the good name of Texas that he was not killed. Now we can't kill him, not after making a treaty with him and he being the only man alive who can enforce that treaty. The only question now is: How can we best use him for the good of Texas and to confound our enemies?"

Lamar halfway assented.

"Santa Anna has told me he does not believe Texas could ever be reconquered by Mexico. Just as Mexico became free from Spain, so Texas should now be free. He has agreed to write President Jackson, asking the United States to mediate between Texas and Mexico and to recognize the independence of Texas. That would end all war."

Though not in accord, Lamar was quick to see all the possibilities.

"The plan accomplishes everything we want," continued Steve earnestly. "It ties Santa Anna to his promises. It would be virtual recognition of Texas by the United States. It will halt hostilities.

"Nor is this all the use we can make of Santa Anna. We can also negotiate directly with the Mexican forces. We can offer to give him his freedom for an armistice, pending international arbitration. I hope to go to the front at once to bargain with General Urréa.

"In this way," persisted Steve, "we can trade Santa Anna's bad promise for an ironclad guarantee. We can trade off a troublesome prisoner for peace and independence. Should we let him keep on setting us Texans at each other's throats? Instead of allowing him to bring discord to us, let him scramble up the Mexicans."

After joint consultations Austin's and Santa Anna's letters were sent off to President Jackson. Steve wrote that Santa Anna wished to serve "the true interest of Mexico" and "the cause of humanity by terminating an expensive and useless war. His manner and his reasoning evinced frankness, sincerity and magnanimity." If he is hypocritical, "it would be an act of perfidy . . . which could not be justified on any pretext." It would give the United States grounds for "interposing . . . force."

It might take nine weeks to hear from Jackson. How avert immediate strife?

Steve wrote General Gaines across the Sabine, suggesting that he occupy Nacogdoches to check armed Indians along the border. This troop movement, plus a guarantee of future mediation from Gaines, might be sufficient to halt further hostilities. Steve begged Houston to support this plea.

Houston eased his leg on his cushion and scribbled at the bottom of Austin's letter to Gaines, "General, I refer this letter to you and can only add that such a step will . . . SAVE TEXAS."

Gaines responded that he had no authority to mediate,

though if peace conferences should be held near his zone of operations, he would extend every help and protection. But he did move his troops into Nacogdoches.

Steve had pulled the three discordant points of the Texas political triangle—Burnet, Houston, and Lamar—into full support of his new plan.

5

Steve went downstream to greet Archer and Wharton returning from the United States.

Wharton was worried about Houston. "He's dangerous. The great victor—out of the swamps. He is secretly opposed to annexation because he wants to be emperor of an independent Texas."

"He is the idol of the army, the hero of Texas, and at present can do no wrong," said Steve.

"Like all triumphant conquerors," Wharton responded hotly, "he will be omnipotent for a time, but not for long."

Steve changed the subject. "Nothing," he told Wharton, "ever gave me more personal pleasure than your last letter from Washington and your faith in me as to the destinies of Texas. For months I have been telling everyone how mistaken I once was about you."

He told what he had done about Santa Anna. "It's too bad you aren't still in Washington to press the matter."

Burnet called the presidential election for September 5. Wharton and Archer rushed to see Steve. "You have to run," they insisted.

Steve was touched. "My health simply isn't up to it. I want to tend quietly to my own affairs."

"Not when Texas needs you so badly!" exclaimed Archer. "That's one job you have never shirked."

"It would mean everything to me to have the support of you two," said Steve. "It would prove to the world we really are together for the good of Texas. But I do not wish it."

Wharton insisted earnestly. "If you run, Houston will keep out of the race. If you don't, he will take over everything. You deserve to be our first president. You have earned it. You know Texas inside and out—from the day it was born. You know how to handle the Mexicans. No one else does."

Steve discussed the matter with other friends. Bell and old-timers along the Brazos urged him to become a candidate.

August 4, in a letter to Gail Borden's *Texas Telegraph*, he announced his candidacy. On the question of annexation, which he personally favored, he would be bound by the will of the people, who would have a chance to vote on the issue.

Former Governor Smith sailed his hat into the ring. Campaigning began. At the last minute Houston entered the race, saying curtly, "The crisis demands it."

6

Charges now fell thick and fast on Austin's head. His long participation in Texan affairs made him more vulnerable than any of his opponents. Everything he had ever done, could be construed as a mistake. The hottest charge against him was that he had "saved" Santa Anna. Hatred of the villain of the Alamo and Goliad ran deep in the heart and soul of Texas.

He replied that Houston had saved Santa Anna. "I knew it would injure me personally to see him, but I did so merely for the good of Texas, for peace, and independence."

He was criticized for calling Santa Anna "sincere." "It is immaterial," he retorted, "whether Santa Anna is sincere or not if, through him, guarantee of Texan independence can be obtained. I am willing to use him on the principle of the public good."

It was charged that he had done nothing but eat excellent dinners and drink fine wines while in the United States. He retorted that he had drawn no salary and had neglected his private affairs. Plentiful supplies had arrived in time for San Jacinto. The medicines had eased suffering and saved lives.

Of all the leading men in Texas with opportunity for accumulating lucre, Steve had gained the least. Only half the lands he had earned by the hard labor of settling Texas were his. He was still heavily in debt for his last trip to Mexico in behalf of Texas. Yet during the campaign it was charged that he had been involved in land-grabs.

"While the land jobbers were stealing, I was spending my own money for Texas. I was in jail for Texas, and the land jobbers tried to keep me there."

He was accused of not having shown due hospitality to recent Kentucky volunteers. "How could I have done otherwise? I have no house, not a roof in all Texas. . . . The only one I had, the little log cabin, was burned at San Felipe. Everything of mine has gone where all my strength

and health and time have gone—in the service of Texas. I
am not ashamed of my present poverty."

Steve had long closed his eyes to stories involving his
close friend and secretary Sam Williams in improper do-
ings. He had heard stories but did not believe them. One
of the greatest disillusionments of his life at this moment
was to learn beyond all doubt that Williams had feathered
his own nest in Monclova like the rest and had then stirred
up the settlers when Steve was still held in Mexico City.
This had delayed his freedom. It was close to treachery.

Williams wrote him that, whatever he had done or whatever Steve thought of him, his own affection would be un-
dying. Steve replied, "Sam Williams . . . you are wound
around and rooted in my affections more than any man
ever has been or ever can be again." But he did not mince
words about "those cursed Monclova speculations." They
involved him and his friends and the country "in evils
which will last for years."

In the campaign, people said Williams was boasting that
Austin would use his post as president to help him. Williams publicly denied this, but too late to do any good.

Though knowing Houston would walk off with the palm,
Steve kept on campaigning with Wharton and Archer. It
was a losing battle. Texas was still disorganized, and many
old settlers had not come back, and many never would.
"Even those old settlers," Steve wrote Perry from Victoria,
are "too blind to see or understand their interest and will
vote for Houston."

Tens of thousands of settlers had rushed in while Steve
was in jail. Many voters were late-comers who had an-

swered Houston's call to arms and knew nothing of Steve's long efforts or of Texas, its history, or its needs. The army was solid behind Houston.

"I am coming home soon," Steve wrote from Goliad, discouraged. "Archer is sick, and I am shaking with malaria."

He would have to live with Perry this winter to wind up his land business, but asked him to start a home for him right away, a simple log cabin—a sitting room and two sleeping rooms, one for a secretary or chance visitor. "Shingle the roof with wide eaves to keep the wet from driving in." This was not the imposing mansion for which he had once made plans.

The election was a landslide for Houston—5,119 votes. Even Henry Smith polled more than Austin, 743 against 587.

7

Steve was glad that he had not been elected. At last he could realize his dream of a cottage, a farm, a quiet life— that utopia of which he had written so warmly to Georgia Hawkins long ago, that he had set forth so often to Mary Holley, that he had seen as he lay on his dungeon pallet reading Plato's *Republic*. But now his health was broken, and the sadness of life had bitten deep into his soul. In spite of all he had accomplished, he would hide himself away half wounded. The pitifully small response that his name had evoked after all these years of abnegation, hardship, and imprisonment was humiliating. His spirits sank to their lowest point. Through most of September and October he was desperately ill in Columbia.

The moment the first Congress met, October 3, it ordered him to report on his land grants. Not only were Texans bereft of gratitude, but apparently they intended to drive the knife into him deep and try to destroy him utterly.

Everybody knew the names of those who had plundered Texas, who had great holdings, who had made hay with the corrupt, crumbling state government of Monclova, who had seized more land while brave Texans were dying in battle at the Alamo, who had enriched themselves in the name of freedom.

Now that his popularity had waned, he was realizing that sometimes the honest man gets his bones picked sooner than the dishonest man, whom small people always fear. Steve had little land left, no money, and many debts still unpaid. He was sick, and his records were scattered or burned.

He wrote Congress that, though it would cost him much time and labor, he was glad to aid in having all Texas land grants investigated.

Another letter came through from Williams. Though much of Steve's defeat and his present sorrow were due to him, Steve answered on November 3:

This is my birthday—my health is improved tho I am still tormented with dispepsia, a most cursed disease for the body and mind. . . . Come home Williams, and lay aside your wild way of talking about people and everything else—harm enough has been done already by it. . . . Williams you have wounded me very deeply, but you are so deeply rooted in my affections that with all your faults you are at heart too much like a wild and heedless brother to be entirely banished—Come home.

27 · Peach Point

HOUSTON TOOK THE OATH of office in Columbia on October 22 at a blanket-covered table in a drafty storehouse, which for some time was to be the capitol of the new Texas. He handed over his sword—"Should . . . my country call . . . I expect to resume it." Thereafter in one little cold room, he dispatched all the republic's business, using his cuff link, for lack of something better, as the official seal.

Houston asked Austin to become Secretary of State. "You are the one man in Texas who can handle foreign affairs."

Austin declined the honor and repeated urging did not budge him. "My health is bad." All he wanted now was quiet rest at Peach Point, free of all worries. His thoughts centered on the happiness of the Perry household and his adopted nephew Stephen. He sent down rose slips from Dr. Phelps, some of Bell's black walnuts, and crowfoot grass seed.

Having no money, he had to sell more land—at the worst possible moment, for it was now a drug on the market. No matter. Emily needed a change. The children should be put in school in the States. "I'll be down any day now," he wrote.

In spite of Steve's refusals, Houston put his name up, and the Senate unanimously confirmed it. Such a positive call could not be shirked. So he did not go to Peach Point after all but set to work in cramped quarters in Columbia with other cabinet members to guide the new nation along its first, faltering steps.

Though Steve and Sam had opposite temperaments, now working side by side, they came to understand and appreciate each other better and easily arrived at the same sound conclusions regarding what was good for Texas. Steve's experience with men and affairs had taught him to deal with all sorts of personalities and situations. Sam had been greatly sobered by war, near death, and responsibility.

The core of Austin's foreign policy, though he did not announce it, was annexation to the United States, the secret goal he had set when he returned from prison in Mexico. The quickest, surest road to this was for Texas to have first a clear title to independence fully recognized by Mexico. This would be helped on by recognition by France, England, and particularly the United States. Now he could push the mediation idea he had worked on before the elections.

When a receptive reply came back from President Jackson, Steve at once had Santa Anna request to be sent to Washington to confer on how best to have both Mexico and the United States recognize and guarantee the sovereignty of the new nation. The bitterest critics of Steve's project a few months before now said his plan was brilliant. Houston not only agreed but appropriated it as his own idea.

Santa Anna was sent north under escort of three Texas army officers. Steve instructed the military men accompanying him to have him ask for his interview with Jackson in writing, and he put on record all the promises Santa Anna had made when imprisoned.

To Jackson, Austin wrote that, unless the United States acted promptly, Texas would have to change its policies and views. Once Texas really decides to become a separate nation, it will never abandon that road. "We cannot remain in suspense. . . . Now is the time or never."

Steve's spirits rose. Once he secured recognition from the United States, the rest would be easy. Others could carry on the work, and he could resign with a clear conscience to tend to his own affairs.

Again his thoughts centered on Peach Point. He sent Perry some oranges, "the first ever grown in Texas. . . . Texas can produce the fruits of the tropics as well as cotton and grain." Steve also sent down quinces, figs, chickasaw plums, granadas, horse-radish, a green Ratama Alsbery tree, various roses, and chestnuts. "Don't neglect them," he wrote.

Early in December he was busy raising more money, sacrificing more land, in order to send Emily and her children to the States. He wrote Perry that he hoped the trip would "restore her health and spirits . . . and correct the fretful habit which sickness and hardships have produced." He could give her $3,000—$500 cash at once, the rest in a

New Orleans draft payable later. He could even stretch
the total to $4,000. He promised to get down for the holi-
days, for it was uncomfortable in crowded Columbia and
the weather was bad.

2

Austin was carrying on the office of Secretary of State in
a half-open two-room shack, windy and cold. There he also
had to eat and sleep. He had been lucky to get any quarters
at all, so crowded was the little town with the new government. Furniture was even harder to obtain. He got some
crude tables and benches for office work but had to sleep
on a straw pallet on the floor, and he had no stove.

In this unheated shack he worked all day and far into
the night, sometimes rarely getting outside at all. On top
of his official business, he had to prepare the report on his
colonization business. He was glad to do that if it would
restore confidence in Texas titles.

Work piled higher and higher, and he did not get down
to Perry's for Christmas. Besides, Emily had already taken
the children to the States. He spent Christmas Eve working
in the fireless office in the shack.

It was a bitter, raw night, and he felt miserably cold.
Presently his teeth chattered, and he shook with chills and
fever. To warm himself, he walked slowly along Columbia's
muddy main street, his head slightly bent. He saw the
Christmas greens on the log cabins, the glow of candle
lights through red tissue paper, heard sleigh bells and
Christmas carols, the happy voices of children. Peace in
Texas!

That was his whole dream. Peace, prosperity, freemen in a free society. He had no home of his own, no wife, no family. But others had homes, and if his plans went through and more war was averted, they would be secure and untroubled in their homes.

Feeling sicker by the minute, he returned to the shack and lay down on his straw tick, wrapping himself in his blanket. His teeth chattered worse than ever. By morning he had bronchial pneumonia and was running a high fever. So he passed all Christmas Day, miserable with pain, his eyes glazed, attended only by his old Negro servant. When Dr. Phelps came, Steve scarcely recognized him.

That same Christmas Day another man lay deathly sick in far-off Lexington, Kentucky—Mary Holley's city— where Emily Perry was expected in any minute on a visit. The colonel accompanying Santa Anna wrote that the river was blocked with solid ice, not a boat moving, and the Mexican general was so ill in his cabin that he might never reach Washington.

By the twenty-seventh Steve was delirious. His head was shot through with feverish images, of things not thought about for years: the old, free trading days on the Red River; rides across the flower-strewn prairie under the stars; Joe Hawkins, kindest of all men; his friend Lovelace shooting deer in the Trinity River brush; Sibley, talking of Tom Paine, his eyes glowing; a candlelit Easter procession up a steep Saltillo street; white goats under the Veracruz palm trees.

Other friends loomed before him: Sweet Mary Holley, so gay and so earnest; Don Erasmo, who had never failed him; good jovial Baron de Bastrop, the old Dutchman. He and

Bell and Steve had laid out this little town of Columbia among the stumps way back in 1823 under the great moss-draped oaks—the town that was now the capital of all Texas—free Texas.

He thought of Sam Williams, with whom he had toiled so many times far into the night, trying to get people settled, working out their problems. Good old erring Sam, "Come home. . . . Come home. . . ." He saw other faces he knew. Bell and his gracious wife. Bell had stood by stanchly all through the dark days. He recalled others who had shared the campfire, the open trail, the log cabin, the Indian fights, the march on Fredonia, especially Colonel Ahumada, jingling his spurs and slapping the rain off his big hat.

He saw again the stately old house in Missouri near the lead mines where he had never returned—never to see his mother alive again. She had been broken by Moses' death. The Austins had given their all to Texas. His father had given his life, too, killed by the long trip through the wilds. James had died in one quick flicker, far from wife and child.

He thought of Eliza back in Kentucky, his college sweetheart, fair as the dawn; of other girls he had liked and might have married, had not things always gone wrong. By instinct he was a family man, fond of children. But he was now, the lonely Secretary of State of the new Republic of Texas, lying here on a dirty straw tick, not a relative near him—no wife, no children, nobody to worry about what was now happening to him. No Christmas dinner. No Christmas cheer.

A voice seemed to come through the mist, and he started up from his pallet. "Did you hear? Texas is recognized!"

It was only a dream out of his delirium, but at that moment he believed it and sank back smiling. This was the goal he had set for himself. Now he could clear out his desk and go down to Peach Point and rest and rest and rest . . . there with Emily and good, steady James Perry and the boys and girls. What a fine lad Moses Bryan was. . . . And young Stephen Austin, quick, dashing, like James had been, his adopted son now.

The drafty walls about Steve, so full of knotholes, turned now to solid stone—green and dank with age. His dirty pallet was in a tight dungeon, and he was looking up at the faint gleam of evening stars through a tiny stained skylight, high above his head, and once more he heard the faint tones of a bugle call and call again.

Or was it the call of the river, the rustle of the river through the canebrakes just outside his door. Once more he stood there alone—before any settlers had come—alone in the tall wild rye and watching the silver Spanish moss kiss the heads of the grass as it bent before the wind over the flower-dotted prairie. Thinking of the Brazos River—Brazos de Dios, "the Arms of God"—he died.

3

In measured tones Houston announced, "The father of Texas is no more. The first pioneer of the wilderness has departed. General Stephen F. Austin, Secretary of State, expired this day."

Houston did not say that Austin had died on a dirty straw tick on the floor of a grimy shack. Nor did he mention the "Arms of God."

Steve's body was taken to Peach Point. President Houston and his cabinet members went down the Brazos and crossed the bayou to Perry's place and rode behind the crude coffin and stood with friends of the old days, bareheaded in the cold wind and mist, in the little Presbyterian churchyard where Stephen F. Austin, who was born a Catholic but whose soul belonged to all true faiths, was buried in a little tomb of home-baked bricks. Words were spoken; music sounded, the rat-a-tat of a drum; and sixteen soldiers, who had been ordered to be "in the neatest trim possible," shot off four rounds of blank cartridges that startled the wild fowl screaming out of the swamp, tossing their silver wings in the misty sky.

Postdate

THE HOUSTON ADMINISTRATION WENT on—a bawling, feuding, pistol-toting period. Once Bill Wharton and Sam Houston glared at each other, hands on their gun butts. The government was constantly threatened by military upstarts. Part of the army started off for Mexico and would have set off fireworks again had not Houston quickly scattered it. Fortunately for Texas, Mexico was too torn by revolutionary squabbles to renew the war.

Progress was made—mails, stage lines, port regulations, Indian trade, new laws—but still no recognition. Texas still stood in an international twilight zone.

Bachelor President Sam Houston spent the last six months of this period on an army cot in the so-called "Executive Mansion," a shack in the new capital at Houston, above Harrisburg on Buffalo Bayou. There—enticed by two clever land promoters, one a congressman—the government was now camped in the rain among stumps. If government quarters were inadequate, other shacks multiplied fast—stores, grogshops, gambling dens, saloons. Houston rarely appeared in public. When he did, he was always gaudily dressed in black silk, velvet, gold lace, crimson vest, and silver spurs.

2

General Lamar became president in 1838. He found the Executive Mansion had only a few battered army cots and hand-hewn benches and tables. Houston had yanked the floors up to burn in the fireplace. Though dense woods hemmed in the new capital, the young government was too poor and workers too scarce to get in wood. Lamar put up curtains.

Just before taking office, he went on a buffalo hunt, camping near the Colorado River. Lamar, first poet of Texas, was stirred by the beautiful rolling hills along the river. It was a high healthful spot, and here, right within bowshot of wild Indians, he decided the permanent capital of Texas should be planted. One foot on the buffalo he had killed— where, later, Congress Avenue would run—he declaimed about the woods and the fine sunset.

During May, 1839, streets were laid out along the 30-foot river bluff above 30 acres of timbered rye bottoms and between Shoal and Waller creeks—"two beautiful streams of permanent pure water," the congressional committee described them. Beyond was a 2,000-acre prairie of "chocolate colored sandy loam."

Soldiers guarded workers who were putting up a tem-

porary Hall of Congress from Indian attack. For five years
Indians remained numerous, and the new capital had to
be surrounded by an 8-foot stockade with loopholes. Con-
gressmen never stirred out of their boardinghouse after
dark for fear of arrows.

It was fitting that the new city bore Steve's name, not
only for what he had done to build Texas, but for more
intimate reasons of which the founders knew nothing.
Once, briefly, he had owned this tract where the government buildings now stood. He had bought it shortly before
he left for Mexico City on his fateful last mission.

From the Aztec capital he had written Sam Williams to
hang on to it for him at all costs. He considered it his
choicest land, an especially healthful, attractive spot at the
foot of the mountains which he planned to use someday
as a retreat from trouble and worry. "I mean to live there.
It is out of the way, and will do for an academy scheme,
with which I can amuse myself and do good for
others. . . ."

But he had had to sell the land to pay heavy debts, to
help Emily, and to live.

3

Sam Houston, re-elected president, pettishly ordered the
capital back to mud-and-fever Houston-on-the-Bayous.
Nobody liked the change. As a compromise the government moved to ragged Washington-on-the-Brazos, which
had fewer accommodations than either place. The Senate
had to meet over a grocery store and grogshop. The House
of Representatives met over a roaring saloon. It was almost

impossible to get a quorum till Houston, now a complete teetotaler, boarded up the inside stairs.

The town of Austin refused to give up the ghost. When Buck Pettus drove his wagons over to get the national archives, the people shaved the mane and tail of his horse and ran him out. When an army officer was sent to bring them, a female boardinghouse keeper, whose business had slumped badly since Congress had gone away, manned a 6-pound cannon and sent him flying out of town with canister shot at his coattails.

The Austinites packed the national archives in metal boxes and buried them in secret spots—just as the people of Gonzalez long ago had buried their old cannon in a peach orchard, except that "the War of the Archives" had no bloody consequences.

By then Austin's dream of recognition by the United States had been realized. France and England and Holland had also recognized the new republic. But Mexico still claimed Texas as part of her sovereign territory.

Foxy Santa Anna was back in power again, hailed as a great patriot because his leg had been shot off in the "Pastry War" with France. He had his leg—the part that had been shot off—borne about the country on velvet in a glass case. Poets wrote odes, orators waxed eloquent, and articles dilated upon it as a symbol of human glory.

He had it buried with full military honors, then squinted at Texas again.

The Texans were getting too uppish. President Lamar had staged a stupid, disastrous expedition to try to seize New Mexico. Every man was captured and marched in chains to Mexico City. The Texan Congress then voted to annex both the Californias and several other Mexican provinces—an area bigger than the United States. Houston bitterly called it a "legislative jest."

Such aggressions had relieved Santa Anna—if he ever had any scruples—of any obligations to keep his pledges about Texan independence and peace. Once more Mexican troops raided Goliad, Refugio, Victoria, and San Antonio.

Houston raised 1,200 men. They deserted en masse at the border—except for 300 who foolishly marched on. All were captured and forced to choose beans. One in ten was the black bean that meant death by the firing squad. It was the slaughter of Ward and Fannin all over again—on a 10 per cent basis. After that Texans stayed inside Texas.

In 1844 James Perry got up a state-wide committee and others in the United States to collect documentary material on Stephen Austin's life. In his call Perry wrote:

He was not only the founder of the Republic, but there is scarcely a blessing which has flowed to this country that cannot be attributed to his untiring efforts for its welfare . . . his wise and prudent councils. . . .

Those named to receive materials at various points was like a roll call of the oldest settlers and heroes of Texas: Buck Pettus, Bell, Seguín, Sam Williams, Gail Borden, and dozens of others.

4

Anson Jones, Houston's Secretary of State, had just been elected president when the Congress of the United States, after thrice rebuffing petitions for the annexation of Texas, on March 1, 1845, passed the joint resolution calling for the union of Texas and the United States.

Texas kept on flirting with France and England, but on July 4 it gave its approval to annexation. A state constitution was ratified October 13. On December 29, 1845, the Lone-Star Republic was formally admitted to the Union as a state.

J. P. Henderson, the first governor, opened the legislative session in Austin—by then definitely the capital—February 16, 1846. Bonfires burned, illuminations were made, drums rat-a-tatted, cannons were fired, powder was exploded on anvils, music was played, and speeches were delivered. The Lone-Star flag came down; the Stars and Stripes were thrown free to the breeze. And so another of Stephen's dreams was realized.

But it meant war with Mexico, a harsh bloody war. Santa Anna drove his soldiers north in another race of death, and General Zachary Taylor marched posthaste to the Rio Grande. The two forces rolled head on near Monterrey in one of the fiercest battles that had ever taken place in the New World.

Taylor lost that battle, but when he was gathering up the broken pieces to retreat north in as good order as he could, to his astonishment the "Napoleon of the West" started moving his forces southward. He, too, was retreating, believing that the Americans, instead of withdrawing, were preparing for another onslaught his weary troops could not stand.

The gray soldiers, the lances, the red pennants, the blue cavalry coats moved, from the shadow of the three notched mountains of Monterrey, south in a stubborn retreat of death and disaster. In battle after battle Taylor moved relentlessly toward the capital.

General Winfield Scott landed at Veracruz and fought his way up through the jungle and into the rich city of Puebla, on across the great mountain passes beside the mighty white volcanoes into the valley of Anahuac.

Nearly two years after the first bullet was fired, the Treaty of Guadalupe Hidalgo was drawn up in the religious center of Mexico, where Stephen had once halted before riding on into the city. February 2, 1848, Mexico ceded Texas and all the vast Mexican region on the west. Mexico had lost half her national territory—twenty-seven years after Moses Austin had received his grant from Governor Joaquin de Arredondo in the name of the Spanish crown. At last Texas was "saved"—if not for Mexicans, for the great tide of American settlers still steadily moving west with the march of empire to the Pacific.

The rest of Stephen's dream had still to be realized. Not till ten years later, in 1858, did the legislature authorize that "a first-class university" be founded in Austin. But it was thirty-five years before it was opened—September 15, 1883. Today with its vast revenues from bonanza oil wells, it is probably the wealthiest university in the world.

In 1910 Stephen's body was taken from the old brick tomb in the little Presbyterian churchyard to the Texas State Cemetery, in the center of Austin, and placed on the highest central knoll under a tombstone with a bronze statue designed by Pompeo Coppini. There he looks down on Congress Avenue, where President-elect Lamar shot a buffalo, and on the handsome modern city that bears his name. Here on the spot where seventy-five years before he had hoped to.found an institution of learning to help man-kind, quite by accident, stand the noble halls of the modern university.

Someday—Stephen had written his sister in 1830—about the time that her boys would be ready to step upon the stage of life, Texas would provide fine opportunities for those with the talents and education to take advantage of them.

For three-quarters of a century Stephen's body had rested beside the Brazos, the river of the arms of God. Then it went to the place where someday he had hoped to escape worry and trouble.

For Further Reading

Castañeda, Carlos E., *The Mexican Side of the Texan Revolution,* The Naylor Company, San Antonio, 1932. Collection of accounts by leading Mexican participants.

Davis, James F., *The Road to San Jacinto,* Bobbs-Merrill Company, Indianapolis, 1936. A romance of the Texas Revolution.

Dixon, Sam Houston, *The Men Who Made Texas Free,* Texas Historical Publishing Company, Houston, 1924. Short biographies of the signers of the Texas declaration of independence.

Graham, Philip, *The Life and Poems of Mirabeau B. Lamar,* University of North Carolina Press, Chapel Hill, 1938.

Hallenbeck, Cleve, *Spanish Missions of the Old Southwest,* Doubleday & Company, Inc., New York, 1926.

Holley, Mary Austin, *Texas,* Baltimore, 1833. Her trip to Texas to visit Stephen F. Austin.

Krey, Laura, *On the Long Tide,* Houghton Mifflin Company, Boston, 1940. An excellent historical novel based in part on the exploits of James Bowie.

Lowrie, Samuel Harman, *Culture Conflict in Texas, 1821–1835,* Columbia University Press, New York, 1932.

James, Marquis, *The Raven,* Bobbs-Merrill Company, Indianapolis, 1929. A lively, accurate story of Sam Houston.

Myers, John M., *The Alamo,* E. P. Dutton & Co., Inc., New York, 1948.

Rourke, Constance, *Davy Crockett,* Harcourt, Brace and Company, Inc., New York, 1934.

Schmitz, Joseph W., *Thus They Lived,* The Naylor Company, San Antonio, 1935. How people lived in the days of the Republic of Texas.

Sonnichsen, Charles L., *I'll Die before I'll Run,* Harper & Brothers, New York, 1951. The story of the Alamo.

Index

265

B